LISBURN

LISBURN

THE TOWN AND ITS PEOPLE
1873–1973

BRIAN MACKEY

THE
BLACKSTAFF
PRESS
BELFAST

IRISH LINEN CENTRE & LISBURN MUSEUM

Abbreviations

ILC & LM	Irish Linen Centre & Lisburn Museum
LHS	Lisburn Historical Society
MAGNI	(National) Museums and Galleries of Northern Ireland
NLI	National Library of Ireland
NLW	National Library of Wales
PRONI	Public Record Office of Northern Ireland
UFTM	Ulster Folk and Transport Museum
UM	Ulster Museum

Credits

When known the photographer's name or collection is given first under each image.

First published in 2000 by
The Blackstaff Press Limited
Blackstaff House, Wildflower Way, Apollo Road
Belfast, Northern Ireland BT12 6TA

in association with

The Irish Linen Centre & Lisburn Museum
Market Square, Lisburn
County Antrim, Northern Ireland BT28 1AG

Designed by Della Varilly Design

Printed in Ireland by Betaprint

A CIP catalogue record for this book
is available from the British Library

ISBN 0-85640-689-9

Frontispiece: Central Lisburn from the air in the early 1950s. AEROFILMS

Contents

Acknowledgements

Since its foundation by Lisburn Borough Council in 1979 many people and organisations have generously assisted Lisburn Museum develop its collections and increase its knowledge of the history of the Lagan Valley area. To all of these thanks are given. The museum, however, is particularly grateful to the following who have kindly given prints or graciously permitted copying of the older photographs that are now illustrated from its photographic collection: William R. Abbott, Ted Alexander, Walter Allen, Barbour Campbell Threads, Hugh G. Bass, Robert Beggs, Richard Bell, Abby Bithell, Griffith Black, Mrs Sally Calvert, Mrs Barbara Camblin, Ronald Campbell, Mrs Adrienne Carson, John Chapman, Harry Coggins, William Drake, Harry Duff, W. Freeman, Elliott Gillespie, Malcolm Gordon, Hall Greer, Victor Hamilton, Mrs Pamela Hickey, Irish Linen Guild, Davis Irvine, George Irwin, Mrs Kitty Johnston, R.R. Kennedy, Mrs Doreen Kinnear, Mrs Kitty Lewis, Lisburn Camera Club, Lisburn Historical Society, Lisburn Institute, Miss J. Lowry, J.H.F. McCarrison, J. McCartney, Mrs Mary McConnell, Mrs L.J. McCurdy, Malcolm MacHenry, Mrs Maureen McKinney, Sidney McMullen, Dan McWilliam, Mrs A.F. Main, Miss Jean Murphy, Trevor Neill, the Very Reverend Sean Rogan PP, Miss C.J. Russell, Mrs Edith Russell (Nelson Russell bequest), George Scott, Ms Carol Smith, S.W. Smyth, L. Woods.

Few books of this type can be prepared from a single collection and gratitude must also be expressed to the following for granting permission to reproduce images from their collections: the Trustees of the (National) Museums and Galleries of Northern Ireland, the Trustees of the National Library of Wales, the Trustees of the Wallace Collection, the National Library of Ireland, the Deputy Keeper of the Records, Public Record Office of Northern Ireland, and the Ordnance Survey of Northern Ireland on behalf of the Controller of Her Majesty's Stationery Office.

Beyond the photographic acknowledgements and those already mentioned, the following people have specifically provided assistance with this book: George Baxter, Mrs Elise Coburn, David Dillon, Maurice Fielding, Gordon and Joy Knox, Kitty Lewis, the Reverend Gabriel Lyons CC, Mrs Vera Morrison, Dr Samuel Semple, and R. Brown Shaw. A particular expression of thanks is given to Hugh G. Bass, Victor Hamilton, Councillor Peter and Rosemary O'Hagan (the mayor and mayoress until June 2000), George Scott and Elizabeth McCrum of the Ulster Museum for costume dating several images. As the deadline loomed and my energy flagged Dr William Neely was also of tremendous assistance, particularly with most helpful discussion of the photographs and text.

At Lisburn Borough Council, Councillor Lorraine Martin, the Chairman of the Leisure Services Committee, and its members, were very supportive, as was Greg Ferris, the Director of Leisure Services, while within the museum the particular contribution of the following is acknowledged: Ian Vincent for his suggested improvement of text and for many perceptive comments on the photographs, Elaine Flanigan for previously collecting, documenting and researching photographs, Trevor Hall for procuring photographs and related administration, James McAlister for his conservation and preparation of prints, Brenda Collins for library assistance and Rosemary Burns for patiently and skilfully word-processing many drafts of the text. At Blackstaff, Carina Rourke for her meticulous care of the project is especially thanked.

Finally the author would wish to thank his family and friends for their forbearance with his distraction while writing this book in the spring and summer 2000.

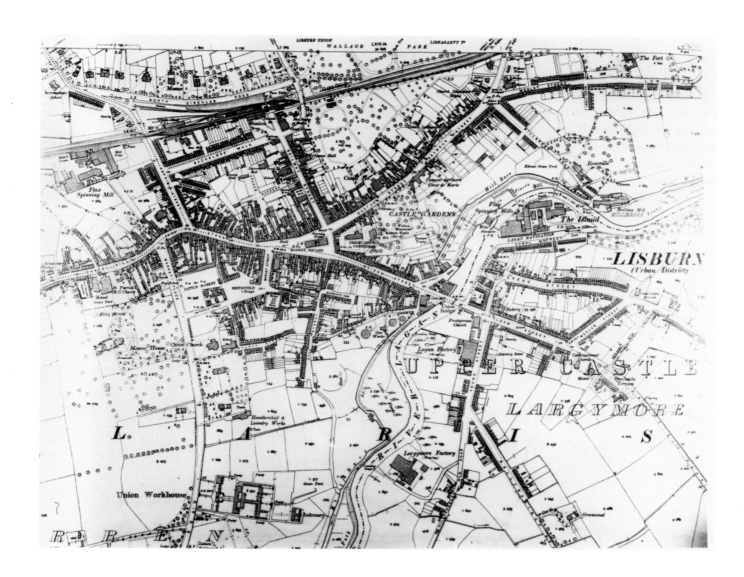

Lisburn Boundaries

In the second half of the twentieth century the urban area of Lisburn expanded beyond the town boundaries as defined in the nineteenth century. For this book, however, nearly all the topographical photographs have been selected from within the area enclosed by either the parliamentary boundary delineated in the 1830s or the Lisburn Urban District Council boundary established after the Local Government of Ireland Act in 1898.

The parliamentary borough included the entire townlands of Lisnagarvey, Tonagh and Old Warren in the County Antrim part of the parish of Blaris; Lambeg South, a townland in the parish of Lambeg that included Hilden and the Glenmore bleach green (but not the village of Lambeg); and the 'suburb' of Lisburn on the County Down side of the River Lagan in the townland of Largymore. The Lisburn Urban District area had a different boundary which, for example, excluded a portion of Lambeg South but included a larger part of Largymore and part of Knockmore townland to the west of Lisburn.

Some photographs from townlands formerly on the outskirts of the town have nevertheless been included for reasons that are explained in the captions, together with a few other photographs of Lisburn people or relevant events from much further afield.

Opposite: A section of the 1903 1.2500 Ordnance Survey map showing central Lisburn.
ORDNANCE SURVEY OF NI

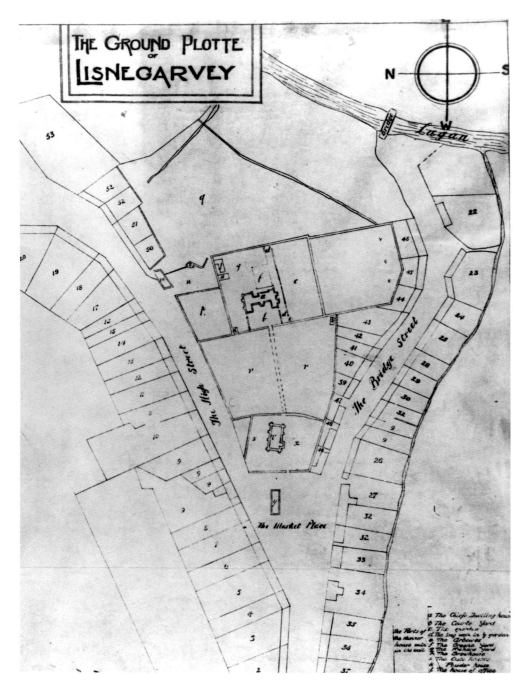

THE GROUND PLOTTE OF LISNEGARVEY

This plan of Lisburn identifies the location of the manor house (marked 'a') as the 'Chiefe Dwelling House', the church of St Thomas built in 1623, the bridge over the River Lagan and a school in the centre of the Market Place, possibly within the first market house. This small town was destroyed by fire in the Irish rebellion of 1641, but the early-seventeenth-century street layout has survived. ILC & LM

Historical Introduction

The town of Lisburn, or Lisnagarvey as it was known until the 1660s, was founded in the early seventeenth century. In 1611 James I granted Sir Fulke Conway the manor of Killultagh (Coill Ultach – Ulster wood) in south-west County Antrim. This large territory of some 50,000 acres, bounded in the west by Lough Neagh, to the north by the Crumlin River and in the south by the River Lagan, had been controlled by the O'Neills of Clandeboye until their overthrow in the Elizabethan conquest of Ulster at the dawn of the seventeenth century. Killultagh was described in 1598 as 'a very fast countie full of woods and boggs' and was regarded by Sir Arthur Chichester as an untamed stronghold needing to be brought under firm control.

Sir Fulke Conway, of a Welsh family with estates in Warwickshire, was one of those soldiers knighted by the Earl of Essex in the campaign against Hugh O'Neill, who had stayed in Ireland to further a career in politics and land acquisition. To establish his authority in Killultagh, Sir Fulke repaired an existing fort at Inisloughan beside the Lagan in the parish of Magheramesk and built a house surrounded by a bawn wall at Brookhill, Magheragall. In the early 1620s he laid the foundations of what was to become the principal town and headquarters of his Killultagh estate at Lisnagarvey. The place chosen was on a rise overlooking the River Lagan and was named after a rath at Lisnagarvey (Lios na gCearbhach – fort of the gamesters), so called because it was a place where the native Irish 'used to meet and play the clothes off their back'. It may also have been on an established north–south route, a place to cross the Lagan other than the ford at Belfast. If not, Sir Fulke certainly recognised its potential as such for he had a timber bridge erected as one of his first building projects. Standing today at the viewing point in Castle Gardens, Lisburn, a part of the seventeenth-century bawn wall, it is easy to see why Sir Fulke identified it as a naturally commanding place to build a manor house. It was reported in 1622 as 'a house of cadge-work' nearing completion, a brick- and timber-framed symmetrical E-shaped mansion facing westwards towards the town and secured by a walled enclosure divided into several courts. In 1635 it was described as planted with a garden and an orchard on the

Jeremy Taylor (1613–67), the Anglican theologian who resided in Lisburn as bishop of Down and Connor. ILC & LM

hillside next to the Lagan, 'a pleasant river which abounds with salmon'. Sir Fulke also built a church on the site of the present cathedral and sought to encourage settlers from England and Wales to erect houses in two streets leading to a market place, the High Street (Castle Street), from his house, and the other from the new bridge over the Lagan (Bridge Street).

At the time of his premature death in 1624 only these tentative beginnings had been made to founding the town of Lisburn. Sir Fulke had no children, so the Killultagh estate was inherited by his elder brother Sir Edward, later 1st Viscount Conway. His service at court as a secretary of state to Charles I must have assisted him in obtaining the royal charter which granted market rights to his fledgling town in 1627 and from then, as it decreed, Lisburn's weekly markets have been held on Tuesday. However, Lord Conway's and his heirs' political careers in London, and their Warwickshire estates, meant that thereafter the development of Lisburn was in the hands of non-resident landlords whose primary focus did not rest on Irish affairs.

In 1631 the 2nd Viscount appointed George Rawdon of Yorkshire as his agent in Ireland. For over half a century this able and conscientious man resided in the locality and fostered the growth and development of Lisburn. In 1635 it was described as 'well seated but neither the town or the country thereabouts well planted'. Rawdon sought to attract settlers. A market house was built in the Market Place and a school established. 'The Ground Plotte of Lisnegarvey', a later copy of a plan of the town from that time, shows that it had 53 tenants, representing an estimated population of around 250 people. In the 1641 rebellion Rawdon led the successful defence of the town which repulsed the forces under the command of Sir Phelim O'Neill but could not prevent its destruction by fire.

That the town began to recover in the 1650s was very much due to the willingness of settlers from Britain, principally from the north of England, to take up the offer of land and building leases at low rents. By 1659, 357 people were recorded on the poll tax. If this represents a population of about 700 people, the town was then the sixth-largest in Ulster. It was, however, in the period between the restoration of Charles II in 1660 and the early decades of the eighteenth century that the town experienced a phenomenal growth.

Lisburn's status was enhanced by a royal charter of 1662 granted by Charles II, as it claimed, a reward for the town's loyalty during the Irish rebellion. The charter constituted its simple church (built in 1623) as a cathedral for the united Church of Ireland dioceses of Down and Connor. Jeremy Taylor, the celebrated English Caroline divine and author of spiritual classics, who had taken refuge in Lisburn during the Commonwealth at the invitation of Lord Conway, had been appointed bishop at the restoration and may have influenced this decision. The charter also established

Lisburn as a parliamentary borough with the right to elect two members to the Irish parliament. It did not, however, create a municipal borough and the government of the town remained firmly in the control of its landlord, who was also responsible for legal jurisdiction through the manor courts. Taylor urged that the Members of Parliament should be selected immediately as 'it would add reputation to us and give solemnity to the new erection of the cathedral'. His son-in-law Edward Harrison was elected to represent Lisburn in 1692.

A leading historian of the period, Raymond Gillespie, has claimed that under Rawdon's guidance Lisburn became the ecclesiastical, educational and military capital of the region. By the 1680s the school at Lisburn 'had become the foremost centre of education east of the Bann', while the location of Lord Conway's company of soldiers at Lisburn was of considerable benefit to the town's economy and attracted several military families to settle.

In the Irish war following the Glorious Revolution, the Williamite commander the Duke of Schomberg recognised Lisburn's strategic importance to east Ulster by choosing it as his campaign headquarters in the winter of 1689. George Storey, a chaplain in his army, described Lisburn as 'one of the prettiest inland towns in Ireland'. Such praise was in large measure due to Rawdon who, with the encouragement of his brother-in-law, the 3rd Viscount, had sought to ensure by careful planning and regulation that the town had a pleasing appearance to match its status. He promoted civic pride and was not slow to praise those who built well or to condemn those who would 'lay out nothing to beautify the town'. Prospering merchants competed with each other to build fine houses to the latest designs, one of whom took down the upper part of his recently built house so that the Quaker architect John Darley could re-erect it with 'a projecting handsome architrave and cornice'. Rawdon also played his part in improving the town by laying on a piped water supply through hollowed-out tree trunks. In 1677 he moved the insanitary butchers' stalls from the Market Place to a new area he had levelled and laid out, presumably what is now Smithfield Square. In 1683, the year before his death, he had the Market Place taken up and paved and with pride claimed that it was the best in Ireland.

Lisburn thrived as a commercial centre with an important trade in butter and hides exported through Belfast. Rawdon, however, feared that rivalry from the Scottish merchants of Belfast would surpass trade from his 'English town'. His concern was far-sighted, for although Lisburn recovered quickly from a great fire (to have a population reckoned around 3,700 in 1725, making it the eighth-largest town in Ireland at that time), it was almost inevitable that Belfast's advantages as a port would lead it to outgrow Lisburn in commercial activity and population as the eighteenth century progressed.

Sir George Rawdon (1604–84), agent of the Conway estate.
ILC & LM

3

The disastrous fire of April 1707 razed Lisburn to the ground. Dr Thomas Molyneaux, passing through Lisburn the following year, gave a graphic description:

> 'Tis scarce conceavable such dismal effects could arise from so small a cause, and in so short a time as they relate, only some turf ashes thrown on a dunghill, which a brisk wind blowing towards the town raised and threw on the shingles of the next house, which, being like spunk by a long drought of weather which had then happened, took fire, and the wind continuing what it had begun, the whole town in half an hour was irrecoverably in flames, insomuch that this accident happening whilst they were at church on Sunday morning, by four the fire was extinguished, and not a house and but few of their goods remained in being.

Another witness, Presbyterian minister Alexander McCracken, wrote: 'Not a house standing, except the market house.' Today the red sandstone arched walls of the old market house within the museum and the gateway through a courtyard wall of the manor house (Lisburn Castle) in Castle Gardens are apparently all that survive of seventeenth-century Lisburn. The disaster drove many inhabitants from the town but Lord Conway acted quickly to encourage rebuilding by granting many of the waste holdings in forty-one-year leases. As Molyneaux wrote: 'If the story of the phoenix be ever true, sure tis in this town, for here you see one of the beautifullest towns . . . rising from the most terrible rubbish that can be imagined.'

Although the appearance of the town was modernised, the original seventeenth-century street plan remained unaltered. Castle Street, leading from Lisburn Castle (which was not rebuilt) in one direction to the Market Square and in the other to the road to Belfast, remained the town's premier street. The road from Dublin entered the town via Bridge Street. Bow Lane remained forty feet wide and an unfortunate bottleneck for traffic to and from the west. The Longstone, a linear suburb of the town, grew up as an extension of this important route, but otherwise the townspeople were largely crowded into a warren of lanes, alleyways and entries south of Bridge Street, Market Square and Bow Lane (now Bow Street). Antrim Lane (now Antrim Street) and Jackson's Lane (now Railway Street) were the only streets on the north side of the town as late as the 1830s.

EIGHTEENTH-CENTURY LISBURN

Throughout the eighteenth century Lisburn remained a thriving market town: 'Grain of every description, meal, and potatoes were sold in the Market Square around the market house.' In the middle of the century, Francis Seymour-Conway, the 1st Earl (and later 1st Marquess) of Hertford, built the Linen Hall to facilitate the town's growing brown linen market. A new meat shambles (market) was erected towards the end of the century, but little was done from the estate's revenues to embellish the town or improve its layout. When the old tower on the market house had to be demolished in 1772, Lord Hertford had little interest in its reconstruction. At that time it was left to the rector, William Trail, a noted mathematician, to arrange for the paving of the streets. The town nonetheless impressed visitors. James Boswell, biographer of Dr Samuel Johnson, wrote in 1767: 'Lisburn is one of the prettiest towns I ever saw. The High Street [Castle Street] is of good breadth and consists of admirable houses all inhabited by substantial people' – by which he meant the town's merchants, lawyers and doctors.

The social heart of the town was the Assembly Room above the market house, an elegant ballroom with large windows, chandeliers, fireplaces and a gallery for musicians. A writer in 1778 sardonically described the 'genteel assembly' that met there every fortnight and the organisation of two splendid balls each year to support the town's County Infirmary. The subscription was 'one guinea per year, and none but quality properly introduced were admitted'. The Lisburn 'quality' were defined as 'gentlemen, clergy and linen drapers' by this satirist, who in the manner of Jane Austen declared that pride was 'their principal foible'.

> A Lady of quality in this neighbourhood came one evening to the head assembly in Lisburn, where none but quality are admitted; being asked her opinion of it, said it was a genteel mob. The ladies in Lisburn were offended, and really from a Lady of the first rank in Ireland such an expression would be rude and impolite: But why should not gentlemen and their ladies have as much licence to despise linen drapers, as the latter those that follow other trades?

In 1785 dancing master Mr McGrath advertised in the *Belfast News-Letter* that he had just returned from Dublin with knowledge of the latest dances and that these could be learnt at his dancing school every Friday and Saturday in the market house. Another annual ball which raised money for the infirmary was that held by the clergy of the diocese of Down and Connor at the time of the bishop's yearly visitation. Dinners were also held, such as one in 1780 when the Irish Volunteer company, the Lisburn True Blues, dined and entertained their officers in the Assembly Room after mustering in the square.

In stark contrast to these social uses was the occasion when John Wesley preached in the market house on the first of his many visits to Lisburn between 1758 and 1789. At that time approximately one quarter of the town's population of about four thousand people would have been Catholic, one third Dissenters (as Presbyterians and the other non-conforming Protestants were known) and the remainder members of the Church of Ireland. Wesley thought that 'between Seceders, old self-conceited Presbyterians, New Light men, Moravians, Cameronians and formal Churchmen, it is a miracle of miracles if any here bring forth fruit to perfection', but his many followers

Louis Crommelin (1652–1727).
ILC & LM

were to prove no less prone to schism after his death. Some three distinct denominations of Methodists with churches were established in Lisburn in the early nineteenth century.

A Presbyterian congregation had been established in the 1660s. Its first minister, the Reverend Alexander McCracken, is said to have greeted William III when he passed through Lisburn in June 1690 and was certainly one of those ministers present when the king signed the renewed *regium donum* in Hillsborough. The congregation's first building in Market Square was erected after the fire of 1707, and the present church was built in 1768. John Gough, a Quaker schoolmaster in the late eighteenth century, preferred its classical symmetry to the cathedral. He praised its interior elegance and 'the large genteel congregation seen there on Sundays'. In this era of the Penal Laws the Catholic chapel was a thatched building in Bow Lane, but in 1786, after a popular subscription was raised by all denominations, an elegant new chapel was erected on what became known as Chapel Hill. In the 1830s the average Sunday attendance at the chapel by people of the town and surrounding district was recorded at 1,200 and a presbytery was built for its clergy in Priest's Lane on a site given freehold by the Marquess of Hertford.

A LINEN MANUFACTURING TOWN

It was above all through the development of the linen industry that Lisburn prospered in the eighteenth century. The genesis of the industry in the Lagan Valley arose with the influx of English settlers to the town and district in the latter half of the seventeenth century, some of whom were weavers. As early as 1671 the town's weavers travelled to Dublin to sell their cloth and by 1697 it was reported from Lisburn that one hundred looms could have been kept at work in the area if finance had been available to buy yarn. The following year the government of William III appointed the French Huguenot refugee, Louis Crommelin, Overseer of the Royal Linen Manufacture in Ireland to assist the development of the industry. Crommelin settled in Lisburn with a small colony of Huguenots including artisans whom he employed in a model manufactory to promote the establishment of fine weaving. Through various difficulties the endeavour struggled to make impact, yet by 1707 Lisburn was described as 'the greatest linen manufactory in the north', before the fire devastated the town and Crommelin's enterprise. In 1711 the government established the Irish Linen Board to supersede Crommelin's role and his patent from the crown was not renewed. His career in Ireland, however, coincided with an enormous boom in the export of linens for which he was given credit during his life time and by later generations who, at the height of the industry's success in the late nineteenth century, identified him as its founder. Of far greater significance to the development of the industry was the

removal in 1696 of the tax on Irish linens entering England, the impact of which was
largely overlooked by historians until the 1960s.

Throughout the pre-industrial period of linen manufacture, and indeed after the
invention of a method to mechanise the spinning of fine yarn in 1825, Lisburn maintained an important position in the heartland of the industry. The drapers and
bleachers of the district, many of whom were members of the town's enterprising
Quaker community, pioneered improvements. They led the movement to regulate the
quality of brown linen brought to market for sale by promoting the inspection and
sealing of cloth. This provoked a riot amongst the weavers at the Lisburn linen market in 1762 and led to the wrecking of the home of John Williamson (a bleacher) at
Lambeg. Local bleachers also appreciated the importance of developing the use of
chemicals in the bleaching process, for which a vitriol works was established in 1764
at the Island, which was created by the new Lagan navigation cutting through a bend
in the river. By the end of the century the Quakers John Hancock and Jonathan
Richardson of Glenmore demonstrated their ability to bleach throughout the year.

The lord lieutenant of Ireland, the Duke of Rutland, on a vice-regal tour in 1787
described Lisburn as 'a large town about which the linen industry was in its greatest
glory'. Its weekly linen market was the largest in Ulster after Lurgan, with between
three hundred and five hundred weavers attending the Brown Linen Hall in
Linenhall Street. Further along the street William Coulson's damask manufactory,

William Barbour (1797–1875),
founder of Hilden Mill. ILC & LM

built in 1766, brought distinction to the town as it developed a reputation for fine armorial table linen, of which it became the largest and most eminent producer in Ireland. By the end of the century it had at least twenty-four damask looms as well as other diaper looms in cottages clustered around the manufactory in the Hill Street and Back Lane area, with a workforce in excess of two hundred people. In the early nineteenth century Coulson's sons, John, William, Walter and James, brought the firm to the height of its fame and achievement. This was assured by the award of warrants to supply damask table linen to the Prince Regent and the royal household. With royal patronage, orders from the aristocracy and gentry followed. International recognition was demonstrated between 1818 and 1820 with visits to the factory by an Austrian archduke, a Russian grand duke and the son of Gustavus VII of Sweden. However, an unfortunate falling out between the brothers after Walter's death in 1836 led to them building a wall across the factory to divide the business into two firms, William Coulson and Sons and James Coulson and Company. The former, under the later ownership of the Belfast Damask and Linen Company, survived using Jacquard handlooms until the closure of the original thatched building in the mid-1950s, while a powerloom factory in Barrack Lane continued the production of table linen for a further decade.

John Barbour, from Paisley in Scotland, established linen thread-making at the Plantation, where in 1784 he built a settlement with houses for his workforce. This gave employment to over one hundred people in the early nineteenth century. A younger son, William, moved the works to Hilden for water power in the 1820s, and with the development of power spinning and twisting the business grew to an enormous size. A second thread mill was built by Robert Stewart in 1839 close to the new Ulster Railway yard, while a flax-spinning mill was established at the Island the following year. With thread production at the Island Spinning Mill after 1882, Lisburn developed a dominant position in linen thread manufacture that it maintained until the second half of the twentieth century. The Barbours had a controlling interest in the Linen Thread Company, an international monopoly combine that they established in 1898.

The introduction of the steam engine, which provided added impetus to industrialisation, appeared first in the cotton industry rather than in linen. The first steam engine in an Irish textile mill was established in Bakery Entry off Castle Street in 1790 in a four-storey cotton-spinning mill built by a Scotsman, James Wallace. The arrival of a 15-horsepower Bolton and Watt engine caused great excitement in the town. A second cotton-spinning mill was erected soon after but cotton spinning in Lisburn did not survive a depression in the trade in 1809–10. However, very extensive cotton muslin handloom weaving continued in Lisburn town and the Lagan Valley until the

1860s. The weaving was largely the work of men while women skilled at the needle-crafts of 'tambouring and flowering' earned additional income from the muslin agents who were said to have resided in almost every street in the town.

LISBURN POLITICS IN THE EIGHTEENTH AND NINETEENTH CENTURIES

In the last quarter of the eighteenth century Lisburn witnessed a dramatic rise in the political temperature that was to reach boiling point in the tragic events of the summer of 1798. The ideals of the American War of Independence (1775-81) stirred the 'Irish Protestant nation' to seek its political liberty. In 1778 France entered the war on the American side, and when, shortly after, American privateer Paul Jones captured a British warship in Belfast Lough – an engagement in which Lieutenant William Dobbs, a son of the rector of Lisburn, was mortally wounded – the fear of invasion led to the formation of Volunteer companies throughout Ireland. Volunteering was enthusiastically promoted in Lisburn. The Reverend Dr William Bruce appeared in the Presbyterian Meeting House wearing his uniform as an officer in the Lisburn True Blues, one of the town's Volunteer companies. The Volunteers assisted in the winning of legislative independence of the Irish parliament in 1782 but were frustrated in their efforts to achieve parliamentary reform. In Lisburn, however, in the election contest of 1783, two candidates supported by the Volunteers were elected, the only occasion in the eighteenth century when the landlord's nominees were defeated. Such was the prominence of the town's radical support that in 1787 the lord lieutenant labelled it 'the seat of discontent, faction and sedition'. The radicals were further inspired by the French Revolution which Bruce's successor, the Reverend Andrew Craig, praised from the pulpit as 'bursting asunder the chains of despotism'. In 1792 the Lisburn Union Volunteers, with both Protestant and Catholic membership, fired three volleys in honour of the soldiers of liberty in France and paraded to the town's new Catholic chapel to attend a service. As in Belfast, a Society of United Irishmen was established in Lisburn, largely under the leadership of Protestant business and professional men. By 1796, however, allegiances in Lisburn had become sharply divided. Those such as Henry Munro, a Protestant linen draper, and the Teelings, sons of an eminent Catholic merchant, were driven towards rebellion by the government's increasingly repressive attempts to stamp out sedition, while others, fearful of the consequences of revolution, joined the new Orange societies or enlisted in the Yeomanry to support the established order. The rebellion in the summer of 1798 was put down with little mercy. Munro, who led the United Irishmen at the Battle of Ballynahinch, was captured and hanged in Market Square in full view of his house. Within two years of the rebellion the Act of Union established the United Kingdom and brought Lisburn's double representation in the Irish parliament to an end. Thereafter the borough of

John Doherty Barbour (1824–1901), eldest son of William Barbour. ILC & LM

Lisburn retained one representative at Westminster until the Redistribution Act that came into force in 1885 incorporated it in the South Antrim constituency.

In the first fifty years of the nineteenth century control of the seat remained in the hands of the Hertfords, whose Tory nominees were elected unchallenged. The industrial revolution in the Lagan Valley and the close connection with British economic and cultural interests secured the maintenance of the Union as the overriding political consideration in the politics of the Protestant majority in Lisburn. When in the elections of the 1850s and 1860s Lord Hertford's control was challenged, it was by candidates who were unswerving in their support for the Union. In the by-election of 1852 the town mob was roused to a fury in support of a local candidate, Roger Johnston Smyth, who opposed Lord Hertford's nominee John Inglis. Even with the very restrictive franchise, when only 230 of the town's population of more than 6,500 were entitled to vote, the open ballot ensured that bribery and intimidation played an unsavoury part in the proceedings. After considerable disorder, which led to the reading of the Riot Act in Market Square, Johnston Smyth was elected by twelve votes. Further disorder ensued at elections during the next twenty years, particularly in 1863 when John Doherty Barbour was elected. He was subsequently unseated by a House of Commons select committee for abducting voters and holding them prisoner at Hilden House until polling day! Electoral calm only returned when the popularity of Lisburn's new landlord, Sir Richard Wallace, ensured his unopposed victories as a Conservative in elections between 1873 and the abolition of the parliamentary borough in 1885.

NINETEENTH-CENTURY LISBURN

In the first decade of the nineteenth century the 2nd Marquess of Hertford provided finance towards the building in stone of the neo-classical cupola on the market house and the fine octagonal spire on the cathedral. Designed by David McBlain and his son, these enhanced the skyline of Lisburn. Nevertheless, the Hertfords generally involved themselves as little as possible in the welfare and development of their great south Antrim estate. The 3rd Marquess did not visit Lisburn during his twenty years as landlord (1822–42) and the 4th Marquess, who died in 1870, visited only once. During a six-week stay in 1845 the latter promised much, but after hosting a great party for his tenantry in Castle Gardens, he left for Paris where he lived and devoted his wealth to the acquisition of an outstanding collection of paintings, furniture, porcelain and *objects d'art* (now the Wallace Collection in London). During the era of the 3rd Marquess and the 4th Marquess management of the estate was in the hands of their agents, James Stannus, rector of the cathedral parish and dean of Ross, followed by his son, Walter T. Stannus, in 1853. They sought to ensure that the

Hertfords' political and financial interests were safeguarded and provided that these were not infringed, did not hinder development. In 1837 the legislative provision for street lighting by gas was adopted and a gas works was constructed at the foot of Bridge Street, where it could conveniently receive coal from the canal quay.

During the Great Famine years in the late 1840s the Lisburn Poor Law Guardians had to provide extra sleeping galleries for an additional two hundred people in the new workhouse. In 1846 and 1847 typhus spread throughout the district and caused the death of two Lisburn men who were dedicated to helping and comforting the sick. Father Bernard Dorrian, parish priest of Lisburn, and Quaker Samuel Richardson, owner of the Island Spinning Mill, both died from the fever while only in their thirties. In 1849 nearly 300 cases of cholera were reported in Lisburn and 92 people died of the disease. The insanitary, overcrowded back lanes and alleys contributed to the spread of typhus and cholera amongst an undernourished population.

Emigration was assisted by a group of citizens at that time, and again in the early 1860s during the cotton famine caused by the American Civil War, when a relief committee had to be established to deal with the considerable distress amongst the large numbers of cotton weavers and muslin embroiderers in the town and district who could not obtain work. In 1863 passage was organised for several hundred weavers from Lisburn railway station, and a further 137 left for America on the return journey of a ship sent over with food by A.T. Stewart, a native of the Lisburn district who had made a vast fortune in New York. The 4th Marquess of Hertford, however, who was at the time receiving £55,000 a year in net rental from his estate, declined the appeals from his agent for approval to give more assistance to alleviate the distress.

Walter T. Stannus lost the agency in 1872 following a vitriolic character assassination by the *Northern Whig*, for which he took a libel action for £10,000 damages, but was awarded only a nominal sum. The accusations raised questions as to the nature of the Stannus administration. The new owner, Sir Richard Wallace, wishing to make a fresh beginning in the affairs of the estate, felt justified in discontinuing the Stannus control of the agency.

CANAL AND RAILWAY

The clearing of the woods in the Lagan Valley in the early seventeenth century opened a great east–west corridor of communications that passed through Lisburn. The town also benefited from the junction of two great roads to and from the south and west, with the former carrying the mail coach to Dublin in the eighteenth century. The opening of the Lagan navigation to Lisburn in 1763 strengthened the town's communications with the port of Belfast, even though the canal was not completed to Lough Neagh until 1794. The town quay at the foot of Bridge Street became an important

A.T. Stewart (1802–76), the New York pioneer of the modern department store and millionaire philanthropist, who was born at Lissue. IILC & LM

11

Offloading coal from a lighter at
Barbour's Quay on the Lagan
canal in the 1920s. ILC & LM

depot for offloading coal and timber and for dispatching grain and agricultural produce to Belfast. In the nineteenth century the Lagan canal facilitated the industrialisation of linen manufacture along the river. Barges delivered the coal that powered
the Island Spinning Mill, William Barbour's vast thread works at Hilden and the
adjoining bleach greens at Glenmore belonging to the Richardsons. By the end of the
nineteenth century the Glenmore Bleach Works was reputedly the largest in Ulster.

Lisburn dramatically entered the Victorian era in the vanguard of railway development, for in 1839, within a decade of the launch of the first passenger railway in
Britain, the Ulster Railway provided a rail connection to Belfast. The town was fortunate that this enormous change did not bypass it, for although not everyone at the
time appreciated the new means of travel, it proved a considerable benefit to the town.
Notwithstanding the furious opposition of those opposed to its Sunday operation –
one cleric said 'its business was sending souls to the devil at the rate of 6d a piece' –
huge crowds turned out along the line on Monday 12 August 1839 to witness the first
train ever to run in Ulster and some three thousand people travelled the twenty-three-
minute trip from Belfast to Lisburn on the day. The railway was completed to Armagh
in 1848 and eventually to Dublin. Branch lines left the main line at Knockmore junction just west of Lisburn, and linked the villages of Hillsborough to the south and
Glenavy to the north in the network under the control of the Great Northern Railway
(Ireland). It was this company which built the present Lisburn station in its distinctive
GNR(I) style.

SIR RICHARD WALLACE – A CARING LANDLORD

In 1870, as Prussian military efficiency overwhelmed France, few in Lisburn mourned the death of their landlord in the French capital. Within a year, however, the reported exploits of his intended successor, the previously unknown Richard Wallace, gave the town a genuine hero on whom to focus its admiration. Wallace, an illegitimate son of the 4th Marquess (though this was never openly acknowledged during his life time), became one of the most talked-about people in Britain for his generous exploits during the Prussian siege of Paris. He used his late father's large reserves of capital to protect the English-speaking community in Paris, and by personally distributing money to impoverished districts of the city earned the popular title 'benefactor of the poor'. At the end of the war he was honoured by the city, the French government, and by Queen Victoria, who created him a baronet.

On 14 February 1873, Sir Richard made his first visit to Lisburn. The town was lavishly decorated with banners, bunting and floral arches and in the evening by fantastic gaslight illuminations. Thousands of his estate tenants and townspeople lined his route into the town and crammed Market Square to receive him with ecstatic celebrations. Wallace was genuinely touched by his rapturous welcome. He had privately stated to the prime minister, W.E. Gladstone, his intention to 'ever be found amongst those who do their utmost to promote the general welfare of their tenants' and was not to disappoint those who entrusted so much faith in his character. Such was the popular mood of optimism that the *Northern Whig*, though disappointed that he

Sir Richard Wallace, Bart. (1818–90), the landlord of Lisburn who made his first visit to the town in 1873. It is unfortunate that no photographs appear to have survived recording this event or any of his subsequent visits to Lisburn. After Sir Richard's death, to honour his memory, the Lisburn photographer William McGeown advertised the sale of cabinet-sized photographs at one shilling each. ILC & LM

should become a Conservative, declared at the time of his registration as an MP that Lisburn was becoming a 'kind of Happy Land' where party political rancour was forgotten. In the early 1880s, however, an agricultural depression led to expressions of dissatisfaction with rents. A concerned Sir Richard, who had not raised rents during his tenure, came to Lisburn in 1883 to listen to, and initiate redress of, this grievance. Shortly before his death in 1890 Wallace offered to sell properties to those tenants wishing to buy, but in the end this was eventually to be accomplished under the government's land purchase schemes.

In 1874, F.L. Capron, Wallace's agent, prepared a proposal with favourable leases to encourage the development of building sites on the north side of the railway line. Thus the area between the Magheralave and Antrim roads saw the building of new Victorian and Edwardian villa residences for the town's prospering middle classes, as well as those who could take advantage of the proximity of the station to commute to Belfast. The building of some '200 workers' houses of a superior class' was also noted by a directory in 1877 and praised, as 'previously the mill workers were huddled up in filthy and miserable hovels free of all decency and morality'. New mill housing was also erected in the 1880s around Stewart's rebuilt mill and in 'the County Down', as the town's development on the south side of the River Lagan was known, as a result of the expansion of the Island Spinning Mill and the establishment of a powerloom weaving factory in Young Street.

It was, however, Wallace's own building projects and his granting of sites in prominent locations for new churches and halls that improved the amenities and appearance of the town. Foremost amongst these were the building of Castle House, his own imposing mansion in Castle Street (the Technical College since 1914), and a dignified courthouse beside the railway station in a design adapted from the work of Palladio, the great Italian Renaissance architect. Other building projects included an estate office in Castle Street and the remodelling of the market house in 1888, thereafter known as the Assembly Rooms. One thousand pounds was also spent on improving the market accommodation and large contributions were given towards a new town reservoir and to the Union Bridge over the Lagan. Significantly, the University and Intermediate School Wallace founded and built in 1880, and the sixteen-acre People's Park he gave in 1885, now bear his name as Wallace High School and Wallace Park. It was not for nothing that following his death in 1890 the people of Lisburn erected a memorial in Castle Gardens with the inscription 'to perpetuate the memory of one whose delight was to do good and in grateful recognition of his generous interest in the prosperity of this town'.

The generally perceived new era that dawned for Lisburn with Wallace's first visit in 1873 relieved the years of frustration under the Stannus regime. Wallace approved the election of fifteen new town commissioners the following year, belatedly allowing the town to take advantage of the provisions of the 1854 Town Improvement Act. In 1885 the town commissioners completed a new sewage system for the town to which Wallace subscribed £2,200. This was necessary as the town's population had grown from 7,462 in 1861 to 10,755 in 1881 and would grow to 12,250 in 1891. Bills were passed in parliament in 1893 for the town commissioners to purchase the market and water rights from Lady Wallace, as all responsibilities for the town's management finally passed from landlord control. In 1898, the Local Government of Ireland Act led to the setting-up of Lisburn Urban District Council with elected councillors superseding town commissioners. Symbolically, they purchased for use as the new town hall the redundant estate office from Sir John Murray Scott, who had inherited the estate from Lady Wallace in 1894.

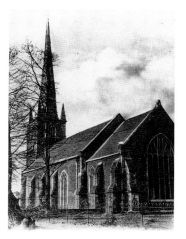

Lisburn cathedral. JOHN LANNIGAN, ILC & LM

THE ULSTER CRISIS AND THE FIRST WORLD WAR

Gladstone's conversion to home rule for Ireland in 1886 caused a deep anxiety amongst the Protestants of north-east Ulster, which could only be reflected in the political affairs of Lisburn. Its large Protestant majority was, apart from a few dissenting voices, staunchly Unionist and ever anxious to demonstrate its loyalist convictions. Members of the Church of Ireland and Presbyterians, employers and employees, middle and lower classes, all found in the Orange Order an organisation to forge unity and opposition to home rule. This reached its climax in the crisis years before the 1914–18 war. At an evening rally in Lisburn in 1912, Sir Edward Carson declared the Unionist intention to promote the Solemn League and Covenant which, with the declaration for women, was signed by over 400,000 Unionist people on Ulster Day, 12 September 1912. In Lisburn, after a united Protestant religious service, the covenant was signed by a large number in the Grain Market between Market Place and Smithfield. The Ulster Volunteer Force was established and actively supported throughout the north. Many joined its South Antrim battalions, which drilled and mounted demonstrations of strength with marches through the town. Notwithstanding this enormous crisis, which threatened to engulf the country in civil war, a few local suffragettes sought by outrage to further their passionately supported cause of votes for women. On 1 August 1914, in the middle of the night, many were awakened by a loud blast that severely damaged the east window of the cathedral. It was thought fortunate that Lilian Metge of Seymour Street and her three accomplices bungled the planting of dynamite, or much greater damage would have been caused. The outbreak of the war in Europe, only a few days after the suffragettes were arrested, eventually led to the cases pending against them being abandoned and the country's political crisis to be put on hold as attention was focused on support for the war effort.

Captain Cecil F.K. Ewart (11th Battalion Royal Irish Rifles) of Derryvolgie House, Lisburn, and the linen-manufacturing family, who was killed in action in the First World War.. ILC & LM

On 18 September 1914, during a recruitment meeting in the Assembly Rooms, 290 members of the Lisburn UVF joined up and were incorporated into the 11th Battalion of the Royal Irish Rifles, a regiment of the 36th (Ulster) Division. Many Catholic men and some Protestants also served in other Irish regiments. Remarkably, on 11 June 1915 about six hundred men of the 11th Battalion of the Royal Irish Rifles who had been making a farewell parade in Lisburn, ending with tea in the cathedral school-house, invited the Connaught Rangers (who were, coincidentally, receiving tea in St Joseph's Hall with new recruits) to join them for entertainment in Castle Gardens. The warmth of the occasion led the *Lisburn Standard* to rejoice that 'at long last Lisburn stood united as one man in a common cause'. However, in the following year the terrible death toll at the Battle of the Somme also united the town in grief as the Ulster and Irish divisions suffered fearful casualties. In all, the names of 266 Lisburn men are recorded on the war memorial in Castle Street. Another war memorial at Hilden records the names of men from Glenmore and Hilden, in the parish of Lambeg, who died in the conflict.

Relief at the ending of the war in November 1918, and the profound hope that it inaugurated a new era of peace, was to be shattered when events in 1920 led to the most appalling sectarian rioting and division in the town's history. As the Anglo-Irish War raged over southern Ireland the brutal reality of terror and counter-terror was to be visited on Lisburn after the murder by the IRA of District Inspector Oswald Ross

Peace Day celebrations in Lisburn for the ending of the First World War, 16 August 1919. The children's procession, recorded in this view, led the way past a dias erected outside the Assembly Rooms. Brigadier General Sir William Hacket Pain, commander of the 108th Brigade of the Ulster Division which included the local 11th Battalion of the Royal Irish Rifles, took the salute from a parade of the town's veterans. The event concluded with a lunch in the Grain Market for some one thousand demobilised servicemen and a sports day and party for almost three thousand children.
JOHN LANNIGAN, ILC & LM

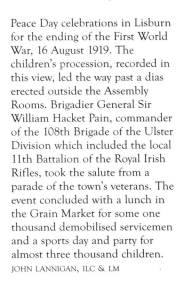

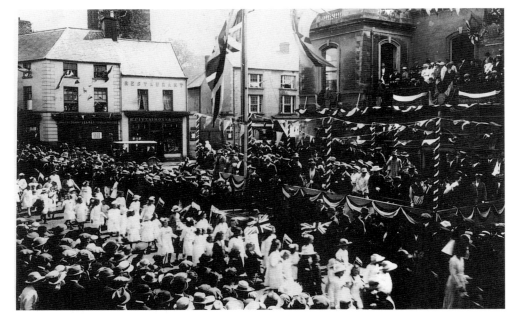

Swanzy as he left Sunday service in the cathedral. His killing was ordered by Michael Collins in revenge for the death of Thomas McCurtain, lord mayor of Cork and IRA commandant, whose murder was allegedly carried out by the Royal Irish Constabulary which Swanzy had commanded in Cork. Unrestrainable anger at Swanzy's murder led to three days of appalling disorder in Lisburn when mobs of Protestant working people indiscriminantly sought to drive the Catholic population from the town. Hundreds of Catholics fled as their businesses and homes were set ablaze. The church and convent were saved from destruction by the military but the presbytery and the Hibernian Hall were gutted by fire. Such was the extent of the destruction through uncontrolled fires that Lisburn was compared to 'a bombarded town in France' and it was a miracle that only one person died in the disaster. Throughout the nineteenth century there had been tension between Protestants and Catholics in Lisburn. Within two years of the opening of the Convent of the Sacred Heart of Mary in 1870 its French nuns bore the brunt of a sectarian riot in Castle Street and in 1874 the convent's windows were stoned after its schoolchildren were heard singing patriot songs on St Patrick's Day. Ten years later questions were raised in parliament about Saturday night drumming parties in Lisburn that disturbed Catholics going to confession. Nothing, however, as remotely traumatic as the 1920 burnings had occurred before. The devastated buildings were soon rebuilt, but not so community relations, which remained distrustful for many years to come.

In Market Square the premises of Todd Brothers, grocers and spirit merchants, W.J. Burns, fruitier, with the Comrades' Club and the firm of R.C. Bannister, solicitor, above, were completely destroyed in arson attacks on Catholic homes and business premises following the murder of District Inspector Swanzy on 22 August 1920. JOHN LANNIGAN, ILC & LM

THE INTER-WAR YEARS

Through the Government of Ireland Act of 1920 that created partition, the new state of Northern Ireland with its devolved parliament was established after elections in May 1921. However, the war between the IRA and the Unionist government continued. On 22 June 1922, Lisburn was shocked by the assassination in London of Field Marshal Sir Henry Wilson, the Westminster MP for North Down. He had unveiled the Nicholson memorial in Market Square earlier in the year and had been invited to unveil the town's permanent war memorial in Castle Street. Peace was restored in 1923, but the protracted economic difficulties of the 1920s developed into an even worse slump in the 1930s, clouding the inter-war years. Lisburn's staple linen industry faced major difficulties through a combination of declining world markets and the world recession following the Wall Street Crash of 1929. Real hardship was endured as employers kept wages at miserably low levels or imposed short-time working. In 1928 it was reported to the Lisburn Employment Committee that there were over 1,200 men and women registered as seeking employment in the town. This included 131 men and 427 women who were temporarily employed or working short-time, but nonetheless represented a high percentage of the town's insured workforce.

In such an economic climate it was difficult to radically improve housing conditions,

Alexander Boyd and Company Limited, a pharmacy, grocery store and coal supplier, at the corner of Railway Street and Castle Street in the late 1920s, around the time its original Crossley gas-fired electricity generator was replaced by Lisburn's new electricity supply. Castle Buildings, Boyd's magnificent premises, were built in 1890 to a design by George Sands, a local architect. The grocery business was closed in 1973, but the pharmacy continued in Railway Street until 1988.
ILC & LM

even though in 1923 it was reported to the council that the 1,040 houses in the town with dry 'privies' posed a grave health risk. Work commenced to replace these with water closets but very few new houses were built by the council in the inter-war years. The councillors' overriding concern was to keep the rates down, but in the 1920s they did engage in expensive permanent road and street resurfacing and in 1930 purchased their first motorised vehicle for refuse collection. In December 1928 the town received its first electricity from the Lisburn Electric Supply Company, which had been formed for the purpose of acquiring a supply by overhead transmission from the Belfast Harbour power station. While commercial premises such as Alexander Boyd's at Castle Street quickly replaced their gas-fired electricity generator with the new service it was to be many years before electricity entirely replaced gas for home and street lighting. The possible danger of not converting immediately to the new source of light was shown the following year when courting couples were blamed for blowing out the gas street lamps, thereby causing a minor traffic accident in Lisburn!

Anna E. Barbour (1876–1941), a generous Lisburn benefactor.
ILC & LM

Water supply difficulties came to a head with a severe drought in 1934, but the council solved the problem for some years to come by sinking a 400-foot artesian well at Duncan's reservoir. It initially sent up some 17,000 gallons of water per hour, which encouraged the subsequent drilling of three more bore holes. The philanthropy of Anna E. Barbour, wife of Harold Barbour, also played an important part in improving the amenities of the town. In 1928 she donated a playground at the County Down side of Union Bridge for which the council appointed a part-time 'games mistress' to organise children's play. Almost a decade later, in 1937, she also gave the playing fields between the Saintfield and Ballynahinch roads in memory of her nephew J.M. Barbour junior, who had been killed when his private plane crashed. The Barbour playing fields were a timely gift, as the council had recently been embarrassed by its financial inability to provide its town of almost fourteen thousand people with additional football pitches.

EARLY SPORTING ACTIVITIES

Organised sport with team games had become increasingly popular in Lisburn in the late Victorian and Edwardian era, a fact attested to by the publication in 1910 of *Sport in Lisburn, Past and Present* by R.C. Bannister and R.V. Hamilton. This two-hundred-page book, with excellent early team photographs, highlighted the popularity of rugby, soccer, hockey, cricket, athletics, tennis, golf and other games. Cricket in Lisburn dates back to 1836, with Lisburn Cricket Club occupying its present ground almost fifty years before the area surrounding it was given by Sir Richard Wallace as a public park. While a Lisburn rugby club won the Ulster Cup in 1888–9, it was association football that was to become the most popular winter sport, with a Lisburn League

A Senior League cricket match between Lisburn and North Down at the cricket club in Wallace Park, 14 May 1910. Grass tennis courts can be seen behind the old pavilion. JOHN LANNIGAN, ILC & LM

organised most years in the period before the First World War. The Shamrock Football Club was established in 1887 by J. Boylan, a future curate of St Patrick's Catholic church. Other early teams were the Hertford and Wesley FCs, but nearly every district of the town had its own team at this time. Hockey also became popular, with a Lisburn club established in 1897 at the Temperance Institute, a popular meeting place for many sports clubs. The well-known Lisnagarvey Hockey Club first met there in 1902. A golf club acquired a lease of the Stannus manor house demesne (between Longstone Street and Warren Park) in 1905 for a nine-hole 'links' which was retained until the club moved to its new eighteen-hole course at Blaris Lodge in 1973. The two local newspapers, the *Lisburn Herald* and the *Lisburn Standard*, promoted a passion for sport and reported in great detail the successes and failures of local teams.

THE SECOND WORLD WAR AND AFTER

As the likelihood of renewed conflict with Germany increased in 1938, Lisburn became the first district council area in Northern Ireland to inaugurate an Air Raid Precautions (ARP) plan and enrol volunteers. This was several months before the Stormont parliament passed an act making local authorities responsible for civil defence. The town, indeed, with the headquarters of the British army in Northern Ireland moving to Thiepval Barracks in 1939, could count itself fortunate not to be bombed during the war. However, many citizens who joined the rescue, ambulance, auxiliary fire and welfare services played a part in the aftermath of the heavy raids on Belfast in April and May 1941. With its close proximity to the city, the town had to accommodate a huge influx of refugees after the blitz. While the government commended Lisburn's efficient organisation of reception areas, many in the town were horrified at the level of poverty of those displaced from Belfast.

Lisburn factories also played a part in contributing to the war effort. The town's three linen thread mills supplied a vital product for sewing service equipment and uniforms. Richardson's of Glenmore converted to the production of aircraft tail planes while Duff's furniture factory made wings for Stirling bombers and other furniture for service use. A temporary factory was also set up at Altona to produce fuselage sections for Short's aircraft.

After the war ended in 1945 rationing continued but the Stormont government began to introduce Welfare State provisions, as pioneered by the new Labour government in Britain. This was to greatly improve social well-being in Lisburn. The National Health Service was of enormous benefit, while improvements in housing began in Lisburn with the Northern Ireland Housing Trust's building of the Tonagh Estate in its modern, and then much admired, style. In the early 1960s it also built the Millbrook Estate in the grounds of Roseville House. Educational opportunities were also improved as a result of the 1947 Education Act, which proposed the introduction of compulsory secondary education to the age of fifteen. In Lisburn this led to the building of Forthill Girls' and Lisnagarvey Boys' County Intermediate Schools in the 1950s and, later, in the voluntary sector, St Patrick's (co-educational) School on the Ballinderry Road in 1966. The Technical College also began a programme of

Lisburn Auxiliary Fire Service at the council's Wallace Avenue yard in 1940. Included, *left to right*, are: Sir J. Milne Barbour, Ernie Irvine, J.D. Barbour (chairman of the council), George McKillen, Alfie Lavery, George Smith, Hall Greer, Gregor McGregor, Billy Crone, Jack Kennedy and Victor Leckey.
ILC & LM (*BELFAST TELEGRAPH*)

expansion with new building on its site between Castle Street and Wallace Avenue.

Optimism at the potential for a bright future was in the air when Queen Elizabeth and the Duke of Edinburgh visited Lisburn in 1953, at the beginning of a new 'Elizabethan Age'. In 1950 the town council, notwithstanding its vested interest in the ownership of the gas works, had replaced the dim street gas lamps with an ultra-modern fluorescent street lighting system, one of the first of its kind in the British Isles and the envy of other towns in Northern Ireland. The growing volume of road traffic passing through the town's narrow streets on the east–west and north–south routes to and from Belfast remained one of the biggest headaches of the 1950s. A one-way system through Bow Street and around the town was implemented but some relief from traffic congestion only came in October 1963 when the M1 motorway was completed as far as the Sprucefield connection with the A1 road to Dublin.

In 1959 Lisburn Camera Club completed a short colour film of Lisburn, affectionately entitled *Our Town*. It took pride in Lisburn's industrial past as well as in the more recent sources of employment, including shirt-making and egg-processing. But above all it captured the character, mood and atmosphere of the historic seventeenth-century town, whose Georgian and Victorian streets had survived relatively unchanged into the second half of the twentieth century. The desire for greater modernisation, however, was to lead to many changes in the decade to come.

A NEW BOROUGH

With town planning very much in vogue in the 1960s, architect and planner R.H. Bell was commissioned by the council to examine slum clearance, new housing and traffic management. There was, however, some impatience with the rate of development. In February 1963 the *Ulster Star* challenged the council, the chamber of commerce and the town's citizens to consider the view that Lisburn was 'slowly beginning to stagnate' and that it regretted that there appeared to be insufficient pride in the town to apply for borough status. The question of the town becoming a municipal borough had been debated by the council in the late 1920s but had not been taken up. The *Star's* criticism, however unappreciative of those who had previously advocated development, did spur Lisburn Urban District Council into action, and in 1964 the borough of Lisburn was created by the grant of a charter of incorporation. The new borough council, with two members of the Northern Ireland Labour Party elected unopposed, appointed James Howard as its first mayor and Arthur Bowman, who had served on the council for some forty years, as deputy mayor. In March 1964, the outgoing council approved the town plan prepared by R.H. Bell. The plan envisaged an inner ring road from the Belfast Road to the Longstone, the total clearance of old houses in the area south of Market Square and Bridge Street, new car parks, the pedestrianisation

The canal quay and Quay Street, c. 1950. ILC & LM

of Bow Street and the development of new housing at Hill Street and the Longstone. By 1966 the first houses in Hill Street were nearing completion, but with some five hundred Lisburn families apparently waiting for houses, questions were raised by Councillor William McGivern of the Northern Ireland Labour Party about the lack of a transparent system for allocation that would avoid canvassing. He advocated a points system to prioritise need but the council stood by its method of allocating houses without discrimination from its waiting list of Lisburn people.

In February 1965 the Lisburn Weaving Factory in Young Street closed. It had produced plain linens for over eighty years, surviving through the worst years of the inter-war slump. Many of its redundant female employees were reported to have been offered alternative employment in a Belfast weaving factory, which exacerbated concern, prevalent at the time, that Lisburn was becoming a dormitory town for the city. The council had severely criticised the 1963 Matthew Plan, which implied that Lisburn was a part of the Greater Belfast area and was equally concerned by the 1965 Wilson Economic Plan, which concentrated its attention on the reinvigoration of Belfast industry. New industries such as the Fafnir Bearing Company, which opened in 1963 on the Ballinderry Road with the intention of employing 250 people, had located in Lisburn, but the chamber of commerce urged the government that much more should be done to ensure that Lisburn remained a separate town and a distinct entity. As Samuel Semple, the chamber's secretary, advised: 'Lisburn's industrial history, its sense of community, its progressive Borough Council, its pool of workers with inherited industrial skills and its independent civic spirit require that it should receive much more beneficial treatment.'

An appreciation of the town's industrial heritage and distinctive identity led to an unsuccessful petition in 1960 that Roseville, a fine Georgian house, should be saved from demolition as a museum. A further call was made in 1965 that the new library in the redundant post office in Railway Street should also accommodate a municipal museum. The council, however, saw provision of a swimming pool as a more pressing need and construction commenced in 1967. Nevertheless, in that year a historical society was founded, based on a groundswell of support amongst a number of people interested in the town's history and concerned that redevelopment was insensitively sweeping away its heritage. At the request of the chamber of commerce the new Lisburn Historical Society was sponsored by the borough council and Councillor Hugh G. Bass became its first chairman. In response to a list of historic buildings in Lisburn published by the Ulster Architectural Heritage Society in 1969, which expressed sadness that the town was taking so little pride in its appearance, few, if any, on the council disagreed with one of its leading members, who said that 'he didn't see many old buildings in Lisburn worth preserving'. Two years later, though protests were mounted, the council approved the demolition of the magnificent courthouse built by Sir Richard Wallace and given to the town in 1901. While the council owned the building, it had no responsibility for the court or library that used it and, perhaps as a result, its maintenance was neglected to the point where it had become seriously dilapidated. It could, nonetheless, have been refurbished for court service if its

Sir Richard Wallace's 1884 courthouse, beside the railway station, was demolished for its inauspicious successor in 1971.
GILBERT CAMBLIN

24

irreplaceable architectural quality had been appreciated. The regrettable destruction of the courthouse in 1971, only three years before historic buildings legislation was belatedly extended to Northern Ireland, was a huge loss to the town's heritage.

In the early 1970s it was a return to the Troubles in Northern Ireland that dominated the headlines. Hugh G. Bass, who was elected mayor in 1970, and many others worked tirelessly to preserve the much-better community relations that had developed in the 1960s, but with the advent of murders and the bombing of the town centre it became increasingly difficult to defuse sectarian tension. In October 1972 a 'prayer for peace', an interdenominational church service in Smithfield Square, was attended by almost two thousand people. In his opening address Mayor Bass said: 'We see so much death and destruction, so much hatred and fear that we sometimes lose heart wondering if peace will ever return to our land and asking ourselves – what can we do?' Several months later the council launched a Good Neighbour campaign in an effort to counteract sectarian intimidation. The campaign was started on a street-by-street basis in the Knockmore and Old Warren estates. Sadly, despite the importance of all such endeavours, the Troubles continued relentlessly. In February 1973 Mayor Bass had expressed his sorrow 'at the death of the eighth Lisburn man in the present wave of violence'. Tragically, many more would be added to that number in the years ahead.

The Westminster government's encouragement of political reform in Northern Ireland in the late 1960s led in 1970 to the Macrory Report, which recommended a total reorganisation of local government. This entailed the replacement of the two-tier system of county and district councils by a single tier of councils for twenty-six districts. From 1 October 1973 Lisburn Borough Council was replaced by a new district council covering a much enlarged geographic area (very similar to the boundary of the old Lisburn Poor Law Union), stretching from Glenavy to Dromara and from Moira to Dunmurry, but with reduced powers. This new authority retained the title of Lisburn Borough Council under a new charter of incorporation. Looking back, the first borough council and its predecessor, the urban district council, had some reason for satisfaction at its record of service and several initiatives that led the way in Northern Ireland.

With the continuation of the Troubles and deepening sectarian division the new council faced real challenges. Amongst significant new developments in the late 1970s were the opening of sports activity centres at Glenmore and Knockmore, and in 1979 the founding of Lisburn Museum. The museum's research and collections have made possible the production of this book of photographic images of Lisburn, from 1873 to 1973. This period of one hundred years, from the coming of Sir Richard Wallace to the ending of the town council, was an era of considerable change for the small but important town at the heart of the Lagan Valley.

Lisburn 1801 by Thomas Robinson.
ILC & LM

Photographers of Lisburn
and their Legacy

There are very few images of Lisburn or its people before the 1870s, the decade from which the earliest photographs relating to the town survive. These early images largely comprise portraits of leading citizens in the form of oil paintings, drawings, engravings or sculptures dating back to the seventeenth century, while the first surviving topographical view of the town is Thomas Robinson's 1801 watercolour of Lisburn. The invention and development of photography in the Victorian era entirely transformed this sparse record and provided images of 'ordinary people', as well as events and aspects of everyday town life that previously had not been recorded.

The best-known early photographs of Lisburn by a visiting photographer were those taken in the early 1880s for the Dublin firm of William Lawrence and attributed to its chief photographer, Robert French. He recorded an important group of town views and streetscapes in the early 1880s that were intended to be published as postcards. He was followed to Lisburn by that great triumvirate of Belfast-based photographers, R.J. Welch, W.A. Green and A.R. Hogg. Major collections of glass plate negatives by these photographers are to be found in the National Library of Ireland (for Lawrence) and the (National) Museums and Galleries of Northern Ireland (for Welch, Green and Hogg). Their work, printable from the original glass plates in these institutions, has provided some of the best and clearest images of Lisburn shown in this book.

Lisburn, however, has not been blessed by the survival of any collection of glass plate negatives by the early photographers who are known to have had studios in the town. A fragmentary record has had to be diligently assembled through the collection of old, often faded or damaged, prints, but unfortunately many of these cannot be attributed to a particular photographer as they bear no stamp or other means of identification. No photographs have been identified as the work of Kirkwood and McGeown, who advertised in July 1884 that they had opened the Globe studio on the north side of Market Square. The partnership may not have lasted, for William McGeown alone is identified as the photographer at the Globe in the 1888 directory that also lists W.R. Ferris of Bachelors' Walk as a photo-artist. Neither of these might have survived in business much beyond the turn of the nineteenth century, for they are not listed in a directory of 1902–3.

Another photographic practice, McBride's, was established at 29 Market Square in 1893, but apart from a fine photograph of Lord Roberts at Roseville taken in 1903 (included in this book, page 57), only a now very faded collection of photographs of renovations at the gas works around 1910 can, as yet, be attributed to this firm, even though it continued until the 1920s. The largest collection of Lisburn photographs by a resident photographer, is, as this book reveals, the work of John Lannigan. Little is known about Lannigan's upbringing or training, but he was in business from at least the 1890s and operated a studio for many years at 52 Antrim Street before moving to 26 Castle Street, where he died on 29 September 1938. By the late 1930s McBride's photographic studio had become McCleave's but was soon sold to Robert J. Fitzsimmons. In 1960 Fitzsimmons in turn sold the business to George Baxter, who forty years later continues to manage a photographic studio in Lisburn. Two other photographers who had premises in Market Square were Maurice Lassells and Jim Shields. The Belfast newspapers, which regularly reported Lisburn news, had, since the First World War, increasingly made use of photographs but it was not until around 1960 that the local newspapers began to use many more pictures in their coverage of events.

During the inter-war years much cheaper and simpler cameras had helped to make amateur photography an increasingly popular recreation. The continuing enthusiasm for the hobby after the Second World War led in Lisburn to the establishment of Lisburn Camera Club, which later had a permanent meeting room and dark rooms in the Temperance Institute. The identifiable work of several good photographers who were members of this club is represented by excellent photographs included in this book, along with others that cannot be attributed.

It is, however, to all the photographers of Lisburn, whether visiting or local, professional or amateur, that great appreciation must be expressed. By their endeavour an important visual record of Lisburn was made that now, through collection and preservation, provides an overall picture of immeasurable value to an understanding of the town's past.

1873-79

Lisburn looking west from the cathedral spire at the cupola on the market house before additions to the building in the late 1880s. The houses in Market Square were rebuilt after the 1707 fire and illustrate the attractiveness of the eighteenth-century town so much admired by visitors. The fields behind Antrim Street and Chapel Hill indicate the compact nature of the old town with its narrow back lanes and alleyways which survived until the 1950s. The Globe studio in the bottom right-hand corner was owned by the photographers Kirkwood and McGeown, but it is not thought they were responsible for this view. ILC & LM

The Very Reverend James Stannus was rector of Lisburn cathedral from 1835 until his death in 1876, aged eighty-eight years, and was also dean of Ross, County Cork (from 1830), an appointment probably made to gratify the Hertfords for whom he served as agent of the south Antrim estate from 1817 to 1853. A deeply conservative and autocratic figure, Dean Stannus controlled Lisburn in the Hertfords' interest until he stood down as agent in favour of his son Walter T. Stannus after the 1853 election defeat.

ILC & LM

Fort House was built by Robert Barbour (second son of William Barbour) only a few years before he crossed the Atlantic in 1864 to join his younger brothers Thomas and Samuel in the United States. His thread-manufacturing knowledge was needed to set up and manage mills in Paterson, New Jersey, which supplied thread to the Barbours' growing business empire in America. Robert Barbour married Sarah Rebecca Edwards in 1870 and is seen here seated with her outside 'the Fort' where they stayed on occasional return visits to Lisburn. The house was demolished about 1950 for the subsequent construction of Fort Hill Girls' County Intermediate School. ILC & LM

Seymour Street Methodist church was opened for worship on Sunday 21 November 1875. The congregation had for some time sought to replace the old Methodist church in Market Street which had served for a century. Sir Richard Wallace, on his first visit to Lisburn, gave 'free of rent for ever' this prominent site at the meeting of the Belfast and Hilden roads with Seymour Street. The church's Venetian gothic style and its elevated design (to accommodate a ground-floor school room) dignified an important approach to the town. The significance of the junction was further emphasised by the siting of one of the Wallace drinking fountains in the centre of the roadway. Wallace had fifty of these fountains cast from a design by Charles Lebourg as a gift to the city of Paris to commemorate the ending of the Prussian siege in 1871. He subsequently gave five to Lisburn, three of which, including this one, were regrettably sacrificed to the wartime demand for scrap metal in 1940.
LAWRENCE COLLECTION, NLI

The old Catholic chapel in Bow Street (now Chapel Hill) was erected in 1786 and is here seen with the bell tower frontage added in the 1840s, which reincorporated above the porch door the inscription: 'Anno MDCCLXXXVI. This chapel was built by donations from people of every religion in this country. To preserve in grateful remembrance such Christian concord this stone is erected.' It was demolished for the new St Patrick's church which opened in 1900.

LAWRENCE COLLECTION, NLI

The Market Square looking west towards Bow Street in the 1870s. The early date of this photograph is evident from the number of ground-floor house windows which still remained on the north side of the town's main shopping square. Within a decade these would give way to new shop fronts and the pavement cobblestones (ready ammunition during the election riots of the 1850s and 1860s) would be replaced by new paving slabs set within granite kerbs. ILC & LM

This photograph, looking east towards Seymour Street, illustrates the elegance of Castle Street where doctors, lawyers and merchants lived in the eighteenth and nineteenth centuries. Partly concealed by the tree overspreading from Castle Gardens is the Convent of the Sacred Heart of Mary, established by French nuns in 1870. Across the street the house with the two-storey Victorian porch was the birth place of John Doherty Barbour, eldest son of thread manufacturer William Barbour and Radical candidate in the 1863 parliamentary election. LAWRENCE COLLECTION, NLI

This demonstration in Castle Gardens by the Irish Order of Good Templars, a popular temperance fraternity in the late nineteenth century who had several lodges in Lisburn, incidentally illustrates the fine terrace of Georgian houses that overlooked the park before Sir Richard Wallace built his Lisburn house in the late 1870s. On the left is the house of John MacHenry (the RUC station until the 1990s), Wallace's estate surveyor and engineer, and on the right is 'Marquis House', a five-bay town house probably built by the Earl (later 1st Marquess) of Hertford in the mid-eighteenth century. ILC & LM

1880s

This handsome stone bridge, built in the 1780s to replace an earlier bridge that crossed downriver in line with Stannus Place, was itself replaced by the present Union Bridge only a few years after this photograph was taken. It was an engineering project in which Sir Richard Wallace took a keen interest. Across the Lagan to the left is a corn mill, which was enlarged in the early 1800s, and to the right the backs of houses in Quay Street. LAWRENCE COLLECTION, NLI

Bow Street looking towards Market Square in the mid-1880s. Note the projecting sign for the Emigration Office just past the thatched building on the left. The Lisburn thread manufacturers William Barbour and Sons particularly encouraged emigration to Paterson, New Jersey, where they found it almost impossible to get American-born operatives for their thread mills. The lion on the right above the shop front of the Golden Lion Tea House was a local landmark until it was blown into the street in a terrorist bomb explosion in 1972.
PICTON CASTLE COLLECTION, NLW

A view looking south across the original Ulster Railway station, past the columned frontage of the courthouse on the left and along Railway Street to the cathedral spire and market house clock tower. The courthouse, completed in 1884 for Sir Richard Wallace, was obviously sited to impress those arriving by train, while the Railway Hotel, with its stable yard, provided accommodation for both rail and equestrian visitors. It was at the station in April 1885 that Sir Richard Wallace greeted his friends the Prince and Princess of Wales. The royal train stopped to allow a brief visit witnessed by a great crowd of the townspeople.

PICTON CASTLE COLLECTION, NLW

John MacHenry (1831–1904) succeeded is father Paul MacHenry as engineer and surveyor on the Hertford estate about 1861 and was retained in this capacity by Sir Richard Wallace. He is likely to have supervised the building of Castle House and the courthouse, even though the former is not thought to be to his design, and would have also overseen other town improvements during the Wallace era. If he was the architect of the courthouse, as has been speculated, it was an immense achievement. His brother, Israel MacHenry, worked as chief accountant in the estate office. ILC & LM

Dressed in butcher's apron, William Drake stands proudly outside his premises at 14 Castle Street where he was in business in the 1880s. He later moved to Smithfield Square where the family business of William Drake and Sons continued as butchers until the 1980s. ILC & LM

Looking towards the market house clock tower and cathedral spire over the roof of Duncan's shop in the centre of Market Square in 1884. The stone plaque at first-floor level commemorated the building of these houses the year after the great fire of 1707. Some ninety years later, in 1798, the United Irishman Henry Munro was hanged directly in front of it. George Duncan, a muslin manufacturer, opened his 'Woollen and Manchester [cotton] Warehouse' retailing cloth and clothing in the house to the left in 1835 but soon expanded his business to include the entire frontage of this prominent and historic site.

LAWRENCE COLLECTION, NLI

The Thompson Memorial Home on the Magheralave Road was opened in 1885 and named in memory of the late William Thompson MD, the surgeon to the County Antrim Infirmary for more than fifty years, who was accidentally killed at Dunmurry railway crossing. Its construction and endowment by his widow, daughter, and son-in-law, James Bruce, fulfilled his vision of a comfortable home 'for aged and incurable people of both sexes'. Over a century later the hospital came under the management of the Disability Directorate of Down Lisburn Trust to provide care for people with neurological disabilities.

COON OF LETTERKENNY, ILC & LM

Sir Richard Wallace, aged seventy, wearing a smoking jacket and holding a bronze at Hertford House, London, in 1888, the year after the death of his only son, Captain Edmond Wallace, a blow from which he never recovered. Sir Richard died on 20 July 1890 at Bagatelle, the eighteenth-century house purchased by his father in the Bois de Boulogne in Paris. He was held in such esteem in Lisburn that the church bells were tolled for two hours during the period of his funeral in Paris and the following Sunday the town's clergy eulogised him as 'a great and good man'. In Paris 'Les Wallaces', as the drinking fountains are known, and the Boulevard Richard Wallace are testimony to his philanthropy in that city but, internationally, he is most widely remembered by the fabulous collection that bears his name. It was bequeathed to the United Kingdom by Lady Wallace, as Sir Richard seems to have intended, and most appropriately opened as a national museum in Hertford House. In Lisburn his architectural legacy has deserved greater protection than has been provided in the latter half of the twentieth century but much remains to be cherished as a memorial to the town's most generous benefactor. J.J. THOMSON, WALLACE COLLECTION

1890s

The Temperance Institute was erected in 1890, on a site given by Sir Richard Wallace to the Lisburn Temperance Union (established 1887, with the Quaker linen magnate J.N. Richardson of Lissue as its chairman), to provide a centre for constructive alternatives to alcohol use. The hall just visible at the rear served as a gymnasium for physical education. True to its social purpose, the building became the Bridge Community Centre in the early 1980s and continues to serve the town in community use. JOHN LANNIGAN, LHS COLLECTION, ILC & LM

YOUNG ST LISBURN

Mill houses in Young Street, built in the 1880s, with the youngest inhabitants on view for the camera. The houses, with the exception of the Eastern Bar at the corner with Sloan Street, were replaced by new houses in the mid-1970s. ILC & LM

The Lisburn Wheelers' Cycling Club photographed shortly after its inauguration in 1897. Racing bicycles and club trophies are proudly displayed. The safety bicycle brought in a new age for the cyclist and cycling became an immensely popular recreation. In the 1890s a cycle track was provided in Wallace Park, where sports meetings were held. An improved track with banked turns was opened in 1953. JOHN LANNIGAN, LHS COLLECTION, ILC & LM

William Barbour and Sons' exhibit at the World's Fair in Chicago, 1893. All the major Lisburn linen firms appreciated the marketing importance of displaying their products at international exhibitions from the Great Exhibition of 1851 onwards, but none more so than the Barbours, who won some twenty medals in the late Victorian era at such events in North America, Europe and Australia, replicas of which are displayed in the oval frame in the display case. ILC & LM

Spreading linen on the upper green at Glenmore, a view looking south from the railway embankment. This bleach works belonging to Richardson, Sons and Owden was reputedly the largest in Ulster at the end of the nineteenth century. Although laying linen out on the grass as part of the bleaching process, as evident from the very extensive area seen in this photograph, became much reduced, it remained a familiar sight to travellers by train between Lisburn and Dunmurry until it ceased altogether in the 1960s.

WELCH COLLECTION, MAGNI/UM

Inside the towelling shed at Glenmore. The linen glass cloths are being washed prior to being cut, hemmed and ironed, and made ready for sale. WELCH COLLECTION, MAGNI/UM

On the finishing floor at Glenmore, where linen is being ironed, folded and inspected for quality. WELCH COLLECTION, MAGNI/UM

A crowd gathered at the laying of the foundation stone of Sloan Street Presbyterian church, 31 July 1899. One of those involved in the ceremony was Sir James Musgrave, chairman of the Belfast Harbour Commissioners and a grandson of Dr Samuel Musgrave of Lisburn, a United Irishman imprisoned before the 1798 rebellion. The church was built to accommodate the growing population in the County Down area of Lisburn. LHS COLLECTION, ILC & LM

1900s

In Lisburn the proclamation of Edward VII was made on 6 February 1901 from the balcony of the Assembly Rooms, where the members of Lisburn Urban District Council and the Poor Law Union Board of Guardians assembled with the MP for South Antrim, W. Ellison-McCartney, and other invited guests. The event was witnessed by one hundred men of the Royal Irish Rifles, their band, a detachment of the Royal Irish Constabulary and a large crowd in Market Square. Following a fanfare by RIR trumpeters, G.B. Wilkins, chairman of the council, read the proclamation, the royal standard was hoisted and the band accompanied the singing of the national anthem. JOHN LANNIGAN, ILC & LM

Market Square, Lisburn.

The west side of Market Square was dominated by George Duncan and Sons' drapery warehouse, which was remodelled with this exuberant Edwardian Arts and Crafts exterior at the beginning of the twentieth century. A contemporary advertisement for this 'busy emporium' stated that 'each Department and Showroom is spacious and well Lighted and for comfort and equipment is surpassed by few city houses'. In the centre of the square, in front of a Wallace fountain, stands the 'jubilee lamp' erected to commemorate Queen Victoria's diamond jubilee in 1897. W.A. GREEN, ILC & LM

Castle Gardens with the Wallace memorial and cannon, a trophy of the Crimean War
presented by Admiral Meynell, former MP for Lisburn. The Wallace memorial was erected by
popular subscription in 1892 to commemorate Lisburn's late-lamented landlord. Castle
Gardens was given to the town council by Lady Wallace's heir, Sir John Murray Scott, in
1901, to accord with what Sir Richard Wallace would probably have wished.
GREEN COLLECTION, MAGNI/UFTM

Irish Fusiliers at Lisburn — Harding, Photo.

This photograph of the Royal Irish Fusiliers parading through Market Square, on a market day, *c.* 1901, was published as a postcard to capitalise on patriotic support for the Boer War campaign. Stewart's thread mill and chimney, completed in 1888 and visible in the background, was a local landmark until its demolition in the early 1980s. Also visible is the new Catholic church built in 1900, but without the spire that was not erected until 1939.

HARDING, ILC & LM

Field Marshal Lord Roberts (second right), commander in chief of the British army and 'saviour of the Empire' during the South African War, leaving Roseville, the residence of George H. Clarke, following a luncheon on 10 September 1903. Included (*left to right*) are: George H. Clarke, chairman and major shareholder of the Island Spinning Company, Mrs Clarke, Mrs Cowper, two unidentified women, Mrs T. Stannus, Field Marshal Lord Roberts, and James A. Hanna, chairman of Lisburn Urban District Council. 'Bobs', who visited Lisburn to respect the memory of Brigadier John Nicholson, under whom he had served in India, later admired the Nicholson memorial in the cathedral. His journey around the town was cheered by people who lined the streets and by a large crowd that gathered in Castle Gardens to witness him planting a tree.

McBRIDE, LHS COLLECTION, ILC & LM

Castle Street, Lisburn's most fashionable street in the early 1900s, with not a motorised vehicle in sight. The railings to the right provide an attractive frontage to Castle House, while those to the left were erected in the early nineteenth century to enclose Castle Gardens. Beyond the gardens the two taller houses were built in the 1780s and by the date of this photograph the first had become a masonic hall, while the second was still in use as the cathedral rectory. GREEN COLLECTION, MAGNI/UFTM

LUNDYS LAST HOUR AT LISBURN

A rare view of a back entry in Lisburn with an extraordinary Lundy ready for burning. The boys are a spirited group of street urchins, from the bare-footed to the better-dressed boy with his alert dog. They seem to be holding some form of torch and have acquired a collection of pith helmets possibly left over from the South African War. Two rather mysterious military characters appear in the second row. Altogether it was a fun day for these Lisburn children. JOHN LANNIGAN, ILC & LM

59

Charles Curtis Craig MP, a
captain in the 11th Battalion
Royal Irish Rifles, was
wounded and captured at
Thiepval in July 1916, aged
forty-five. ILC & LM

The Union Bridge as built in the 1880s to replace an earlier bridge over the River Lagan. On
the evening of 22 January 1906 Charles Curtis Craig, MP for South Antrim, first elected in
1903, met his younger brother, Captain James Craig, the new MP for East Down (the
constituency stretched from Downpatrick to Lisburn), on the middle of the bridge to

Captain James Craig MP, who with Sir Edward Carson was to lead Unionist resistance to home rule for Ireland, is shown as an officer of the Royal Irish Rifles during his service in the South African War. He enlisted again with his brother Charles in 1914. ILC & LM

celebrate their successful candidature as Unionists in the 1906 general election. The event, stage-managed at the point where their two constituencies joined, was witnessed by a large crowd of their respective Lisburn constituents from both sides of the River Lagan.
GREEN COLLECTION, MAGNI/UFTM

THE MARKET PLACE, LISBURN.   WAG 223

A charming photograph of the junction of Market Place with Bow Street in the age of farm carts. The Wallace fountain had its use for the weary. GREEN COLLECTION, MAGNI/UFTM

Market Street in the early twentieth century. The hall to the right of McFadden's was the first Methodist chapel in Lisburn in which John Wesley preached in 1789. Between 1912 and 1927 it was the Electric Picture Palace, where the first show was *The Charge of the Light Brigade*. It later returned to religious use as the Christian Workers' Union Hall. The woman in the black shawl at the doorway of McFadden's appears as many mill workers would have been dressed in the period. ILC & LM

An early-twentieth-century photograph of R.J. Allen's second-hand shop at 70 Bridge Street, now demolished. The narrow entrance under the lamp is to Edgar's Entry where, in 1862, eleven families lived huddled in very small dwellings. Such entries, once common in Bridge Street and around the town, provided unhealthy living conditions and were death traps in the event of fire. By the inter-war years Edgar's Entry, or Sloan's Entry as it became known, was in use as workshops and stores for Allen's shop and no longer inhabited. ILC & LM

The staff of the County Antrim Infirmary in the early 1900s, including (front row) the surgeon, Dr George St George MD, and the matron, Miss Melville, and in the back row an apprentice surgeon, Dr J.G. Johnston. Referring to Dr St George's appointment in 1882, the *Lisburn Standard* commented that in the absence of antiseptics abdominal operations were rarely attempted – though by the date of this photograph both had become commonplace.
JOHN LANNIGAN, ILC & LM

The County Antrim Infirmary, established in Bow Lane in 1767, was removed to this building in Seymour Street in the early 1800s. The hospital was much improved in Dr St George's era with financial assistance from the Barbour family and other benefactors. It received an extensive internal modernisation in 1913 (when this view was taken) following a bazaar that raised £1,350. New facilities included the installation of electric power for lighting, a lift, and the improvement of X-ray apparatus, and also an enlarged operating theatre. A house for nursing staff accommodation (to the left) had also been purchased.

BELFAST TELEGRAPH

Above: An Edwardian photograph of the staff and pupils of the Ulster Provincial (Friends') School. Founded by the will of John Hancock, a Lisburn Quaker, and opened in 1774, this school overlooked the town from its original site at Prospect Hill. The school, which began to enrol non-Quaker pupils shortly after the date of this photograph, has played an important part in the educational life of the town. ILC & LM

Opposite bottom: Primrose Football Club had a team that played in the first Lisburn League in 1893–4. This photograph is of the all-conquering 1909–10 side which won the *Lisburn Standard* League Cup and defeated Roseville (Millbrook district) before a large crowd to win the McCloy Cup. The third trophy might be the Dr George St George Charity Cup, which was played for to raise money for the County Antrim Infirmary. ILC & LM

An early photograph of the first members of Lisnagarvey Hockey Club, in their original dark blue shirts with a diagonal light blue stripe, taken within a year or two of the club's foundation in September 1902. Both R.C. (Bob) Bannister (standing, sixth from left) and W.S. (Wally) Duncan (standing, fourth from left) had the honour of being captain in the club's first season, for they exchanged their elected offices part way through the year, with Bannister taking the secretaryship, a position he was to hold for many years. F.G. (Fred) Hull (seated, first left) was, in the 1907–8 season, the first Lisburn man to play for Ireland and later, in the 1914–18 war, served as an officer in the 11th Battalion of the Royal Irish Rifles. The club won the Minor League in the 1904–5 season and the Junior League and Cup in the 1906–7 season. In the decades ahead 'Garvey' went on to become one of the best-known and most successful senior clubs in Irish hockey. JOHN LANNIGAN, LHS COLLECTION, ILC & LM

1910s

MARKET DAY IN LISBURN, LET EM ALL COME" WAG 117

These two photographs from the 1910s capture the atmosphere of the bustling weekly Tuesday general market which took place in Market Square. Delph and crockery, including 'present from Lisburn' ware, drapery and household hardware were sought after by town and country people who flocked to the market in search of bargains. The rough-and-tumble stalls are in contrast to the orderly display of fashionable clothes in the first-floor windows of

MARKET DAY IN LISBURN, LADIES' OUTFITTING DEPARTMENT   WAG 1172

George Duncan's drapery warehouse. *Above:* Smoke rises from Stewart's mill chimney, the top of which is hidden by the lantern of the 'jubilee lamp'. In the 1930s the general market was relocated from Market Square to the Smithfield area, where it has continued to the present day. GREEN COLLECTION, MAGNI/UFTM

A gathering of family and friends at the *Lisburn Herald* printing works in the yard behind the newspaper's offices at 32 Bow Street. Established in 1891 by Robert McMullen, the *Herald* remained in operation under the editorship of James McCarrison (not present here) and later his son Harold, until its closure in 1969. On 22 June 1911 Robert McMullen was awarded the town's first prize for the decoration of his premises during the celebrations for the coronation of George V. This photograph could have been taken at that time or some years earlier during another festive occasion. ILC & LM

John Magill's licensed premises and funeral undertaking business at 8 Market Square (now Woodside's department store) is here seen decorated for an unidentified royal occasion, possibly the coronation of George V in 1911. Magill's was on the site of the King's Arms, an inn and stop for horse-drawn coaches on the route between Belfast and Armagh. The significance and names of those included with the horses and the goat has sadly not been recorded.

ILC & LM

Lisburn Co-Operative Society premises adjoining the town hall, Castle Street, in the 1910s. Established in 1882, 'the Co-op' was of great benefit to the people of the town. Young married couples were encouraged to join, 'as a means of providing a pension for old age and as an assurance for their homes being provided with goods of best quality'. The society was amalgamated with the Working Men's Club in 1905 and, with its billiard tables, shooting range, library and brass band, also served as a recreational organisation. Harold Barbour, its first president, was a friend of Sir Horace Plunkett, founder and promoter of the co-operative movement in Ireland. ILC & LM

Lisnagarvey Ladies' Hockey Club, 1912. A ladies' team was first established in 1904 as a branch of the men's club, with whom mixed matches were often played as they proved very popular. In the 1904–5 season Lisnagarvey won the Junior Cup but, after a difficult season in Senior League, interest waned and the club became dormant until it was re-established by this team in 1911. The club had a particularly successful team in the 1920s when Kitty and Sylvia Kirkwood, the daughters of its first captain, Mrs Hugh Kirkwood, also played for Ireland. ILC & LM

The related Harvey and Maxwell families ran this very typical late-Victorian-styled spirit grocer's in an eighteenth-century building in Market Square, which still survives though no longer as a public house. ILC & LM

The wooden Orange arch erected by Lodge No. 111 (Lower Maze), decorated with shavings coloured in the Island Spinning Mill dye house, at the time of the anti-home rule agitation before the First World War. Only a few of those present have been identified: *left to right*: Sam McMullen, son of the owner of the *Lisburn Herald*, standing on the oil drum; standing on the road, Richard and Joseph McCartney, caulkers at Harland and Wolff, fifth and ninth men, and Thomas McCartney, printer at the *Herald*, eleventh man; and Harry Lyttle, plumber, extreme right. ILC & LM

The Derriaghy Unionist Club drilling with wooden rifles in front of Ballymacash House, c. 1912, with the formidable bearded figure of seventy-three-year-old Canon J.A. Stewart standing in the centre. Canon Stewart, who died the following year, was a generous supporter of the Lisburn Temperence Institute and a major benefactor of the County Antrim Infirmary. ILC & LM

The machine gun company of the 1st Battalion of the South Antrim Ulster Volunteer Force at North Circular Road, probably after the gun-running on 1 May 1914 and shortly before the outbreak of the First World War. *Left to right:* William Wilson, John Smyth, Tom Hanna, Hugh Burrowes, Robert Lavery, James Bell, Artie Burrowes, Harry Bell (holding the horse), William Jefferson (machine gunner), John McGann, William Bell, James Morrison, James Abbott, and Robert C. Browne. JOHN LANNIGAN, ILC & LM

The 1st Battalion South Antrim UVF in the Grain Market (note the tower of Christ Church parish church almost hidden by the trees in the background), showing (*left to right*), the machine gun section, dispatch riders with an extraordinary rocket-shaped motorbike side car, and horse-drawn transport at the rear, prior to setting out for manoeuvres at the White Mountain on 4 August 1914. JOHN LANNIGAN, ILC & LM

Looking down Bow Street from Market Square in the 1910s. To the right the three-balled sign denotes Pelan's, one of the local pawnbrokers, and a place of importance to the town's poor; and, on the left, Hugh Kirkwood's hardware and ironmongery store in an eighteenth-century building embellished in the late Victorian fashion. It was there in 1914 that suffragette Mrs Metge amazingly tried to buy dynamite, which she claimed was to dislodge a tree stump in her garden. Her failure to procure it without a licence did not prevent the cathedral bomb outrage some weeks later. GREEN COLLECTION, MAGNI/UFTM

The Georgian sedan chair of William Coulson decorated with flax for the marriage of handloom weaver William Bunter in 1915, who appears somewhat abashed. Presumably the woman is his bride-to-be. The use of this chair (now in the collection of the Ulster Folk and Transport Museum) to celebrate a marriage was a tradition of William Coulson and Sons, damask manufacturers. ILC & LM

The new Municipal Technical Institute in Castle Street, shown with its students, some time after its opening in 1914. Formerly Castle House, the Lisburn residence of Sir Richard Wallace built in 1880, it was stripped of its eighteenth-century fireplaces, tapestries, furniture and other *objects d'art* by Sir John Murray Scott and left unoccupied until Lisburn Urban District Council purchased it to provide a college for technical education. Cecil Webb, its first distinguished principal, who served until 1941, is immediately to the left of the balcony doorway. ILC & LM

The courthouse, photographed at the end of the decade, when the suffragettes were brought to trial following the cathedral bomb outrage on 1 August 1914. Here, Lilian Metge boldly declared 'there is one law for women and another for men'. The headlines in the *Lisburn Standard* read 'Suffragette Antics in Lisburn Court' and 'Wild Women Released'. ILC & LM

A record of a farewell celebration in 1914–15 outside Tom Oliver's public house at the corner of Bow Street and Antrim Street. How many came back? JOHN LANNIGAN, ILC & LM

Bugler W.J. Bingham, 11th Battalion Royal
Irish Rifles, photographed in Lisburn in 1915.
He was wounded at the Battle of the Somme
on 1 July 1916. JOHN LANNIGAN, ILC & LM

The Abbott brothers, James, Thomas and William, of 15 McKeown Street, photographed at the Crimean cannon in Castle Gardens in 1915. The three brothers were members of the South Antrim UVF who joined the 11th Battalion Royal Irish Rifles and fought at the Battle of the Somme. The youngest brother, Rifleman William Abbott, was killed on 1 July 1916.
JOHN LANNIGAN, ILC & LM

The presentation of a 'loving cup' to Lieutenant Nelson Russell in the town hall,
15 September 1916. Born in Lisburn in 1897, Nelson Russell joined the Royal Irish Fusiliers
in 1914. The award of a Military Cross for his command of a daring daylight raid of the
German trenches at the Somme on 17 April 1916 led to this reception being organised in
his honour. Seated at the table are Lady Richardson, General Sir George Richardson,
Lieutenant Nelson Russell, J.S.F.M. McCance, chairman of Antrim County Council, and
James McCarrison, editor of the *Lisburn Herald*. Standing are J.G. Ferguson, J.A. Hanna,
J. Carson, H. Kirkwood, G. Dunlop, Mrs Stalker, Mrs Duncan, J. Stalker, G. Duncan,
Harold Barbour, Thomas Sinclair (chairman of the meeting), Nelson Russell senior, Mrs
Russell, Canon Banks, and H. Russell. JOHN LANNIGAN, ILC & LM

The wooden cenotaph erected in Market Square for the Peace Day celebrations on
16 August 1919. Posted at the four corners of the cenotaph were soldiers with their heads
bowed and arms reversed as the parade passed by. This temporary memorial was constructed
by Ezekial Bullick, the owner of a local joinery firm, in a design similar to that of the
cenotaph in Whitehall, London. JOHN LANNIGAN, ILC & LM

1920s

The planting of a 'peace tree' in the grounds of the workhouse (now Lagan Valley Hospital) by Lady Keightley, chairman of the Board of Guardians (1913–20), 3 February 1920. The photograph illustrates the predominance of male members of a board on which Louisa Stannus, the woman on the extreme right, was the only other female member in the 1920s. The election of women to the twenty-six-member board continued to be a rarity despite an appeal by Anna E. Barbour who asserted, on her retirement as a guardian in 1912, that it was 'essentially a woman's work'. The dedicated service of Gertrude Keightley, wife of Sir Samuel, whose son Captain Philip Keightley was killed in the 1914–18 war, was exceptional. In 1907 she was commended by a government inspector for developing the high standards of foster homes in the area through single-handedly selecting these and making follow-up visits to ensure continuing good care of orphans and abandoned children.

ILC & LM (*BELFAST TELEGRAPH*)

The Northern Bank at the corner of Market Square and Railway Street, outside which District Inspector Oswald Ross Swanzy, RIC, was shot on Sunday 22 August 1920 *en route* to his house in Railway Street. His murder was the spark that ignited the flames of the burnings during the most awful sectarian riots in the history of Lisburn. JOHN LANNIGAN, ILC & LM

Public houses such as Thomas Browne's were looted, and drunkenness added to the fury of the mob following the Swanzy murder. Thomas Browne, a young publican who had settled in Lisburn only a year or two before, is looking out from the gateway. He subsequently repaired his damaged premises, married and raised a family in the accommodation above the public house. ILC & LM

Premises in Bow Street completely destroyed in the riots. Despite the sectarian conflict, a Catholic nun is making her way unescorted through the town. ILC & LM

The completely gutted Catholic presbytery in Priest's Lane (now Tonagh Avenue) off Longstone Street following the Swanzy riots. The present parochial house was built beside St Patrick's church on Chapel Hill in the mid-1920s.
ILC & LM

Looking down Longstone Street towards Chapel Hill. To the right can be seen a terrace of white-washed thatched cottages gutted by fire in the burning of Catholic homes in August 1920. JOHN LANNIGAN, ILC & LM

Children playing in buildings laid waste on Chapel Hill after the burnings of August 1920. ILC & LM

91

'Kentuckey Bar off Antrim Street. Remnants of the loot' was the photographer's caption for this willing cast of outlaws, shamelessly posing with alcohol looted from public houses during the burnings and riots of August 1920. JOHN LANNIGAN, ILC & LM

The Convent of the Sacred Heart of Mary in Castle Street under armed guard during the disturbances of August 1920. The two 'tommies' on duty are standing beside the telegraph pole. The convent closed in 1970 and the building was subsequently demolished.

BELFAST TELEGRAPH

'Success to our Ulster Parliament': Lisburn Orange Hall, Railway Street (built 1871),
decorated to celebrate the opening of the new Northern Ireland parliament in Belfast City
Hall, June 1921. JOHN LANNIGAN, ILC & LM

Sir James Craig, prime minister of Northern Ireland, speaking at the unveiling of the
Nicholson memorial in Market Square, 19 January 1922. Seated are: the soon-to-be-
assassinated Field Marshal Sir Henry Wilson, Chief of the Imperial General Staff since 1917,
then just retired, who had been invited to unveil the memorial, and Dr George St George,
chairman of Lisburn Urban District Council. LHS COLLECTION, ILC & LM

A detachment of 'A' class Special Constabulary present arms while the last post is sounded beneath the statue of Brigadier General John Nicholson at a ceremony on 11 December 1922 to mark the centenary of his birth. Nicholson, a Victorian hero who grew up in his mother's home town of Lisburn, was killed leading the assault on Delhi in 1857, aged thirty-five years. The statue, to a design by F.W. Pomeroy, had been gifted by Henry Musgrave, the Lisburn-born benefactor of Belfast who died in January 1922, only weeks before it was unveiled. ILC & LM

John Milne Barbour addresses spectators at the unveiling of the war memorial in Castle Gardens, 28 April 1923. The memorial was unveiled by Major General Sir Oliver Nugent, a commander of the Ulster Division. Colonel H.A. Pakenham read aloud the names of 266 Lisburn men who died in the 1914–18 war. In the foreground, in front of the ranks of the Seaforth Highlanders, standing in the 'at ease' position, are ranks of local men who had served. The sculpted war memorial is by H.C. Fehr. ILC & LM

An illicit still for making poteen discovered on the premises of J. Bailey, Antrim Road, and proudly displayed by the police in this early 1920s photograph. Such stills were not uncommon in Irish towns at this period. JOHN LANNIGAN, ILC & LM

Hilden House, built by William Barbour in 1823 when he purchased a former bleach green on the banks of the River Lagan to take advantage of water power for his new thread mill. The house is shown with its Victorian veranda a century later. ILC & LM

The Reverend Robert Wilson Hamilton (1851–1935), minister of Railway Street Presbyterian church from 1885 to 1930 and senior minister until his death, seen here in his robes as Moderator of the General Assembly. R.W. Hamilton, an evangelical pastor, was an ardent temperance campaigner who played a leading role in founding and supporting the Lisburn Temperance Union. He twice addressed political meetings in opposition to the Craig brothers, Charles and James, as he believed the sons of a distiller were not fit to represent people in parliament. He particularly resented their provision of free alcohol in Lisburn public houses during the 1903 and 1906 eletion campaigns. As a convinced Liberal, Hamilton faced some political hostility in Lisburn but was never afraid to express his views. During his moderatorship (1924–5), in a speech in Dublin, he declared that 'if Mr Gladstone's Home Rule Bill had become law we would not have had the deplorable lawlessness and strife and murders that had so blackened our history'. This led to his denunciation in some Belfast newspapers and an extensive correspondence both for and against his point of view. ILC & LM

The dinner given in the town hall by Lisburn Urban District Council for Milne Barbour, grandson of William Barbour and chairman of the Linen Thread Company, on his appointment as minister of commerce in the government of Northern Ireland, 7 May 1925. A.R. HOGG, ILC & LM

Captain Charles C. Craig, Westminster MP for South Antrim from 1903 to 1929 and brother of Sir James Craig, is seen speaking at the opening of South Antrim Hockey Club's new pavilion at its ground near Prospect Hill, 10 October 1925. The opening ceremony, performed by Sir Robert Baird, managing director of the *Belfast Telegraph* (seated reading notes), took place at half-time during a Senior League match between Lisnagarvey and South Antrim. Sir Robert described Lisburn, with its two successful clubs, as 'the hub of hockey in Ulster, if not Ireland'. Also included are: the Very Reverend R.W. Hamilton (in a top hat) and to the right of Baird, Milne Barbour, patron of South Antrim Hockey Club, and his sister-in-law Anna E. Barbour. Councillor J.G. Hanna, who represented Lisburn Urban District Council, is seated at the extreme right. ILC & LM (*BELFAST TELEGRAPH*)

William Coulson's original damask manufactory, built in 1766 in Linenhall Street, which continued in operation in this thatched building until the mid-1950s. In this cottage-like factory fine armorial table linen was woven for George III, the Prince Regent, Queen Victoria and other distinguished customers throughout Europe. It was finally demolished in 1966, an irreplaceable loss to Lisburn's heritage. ILC & LM

A damask handloom weaver at work at a Jacquard tablecloth loom inside the original Coulson's thatched factory in Linenhall Street. WELCH COLLECTION, MAGNI/UM

'Twisting on' a new warp to a damask tablecloth loom in one of the two Coulson factories in 1925. The ratchet wheel with its crowned harp probably identifies this loom as one of those grant-aided by the Irish Linen Board in the early nineteenth century. The pattern holes in the Jacquard cards can be clearly seen in the card loft above the loom. A.R. HOGG, ILC & LM

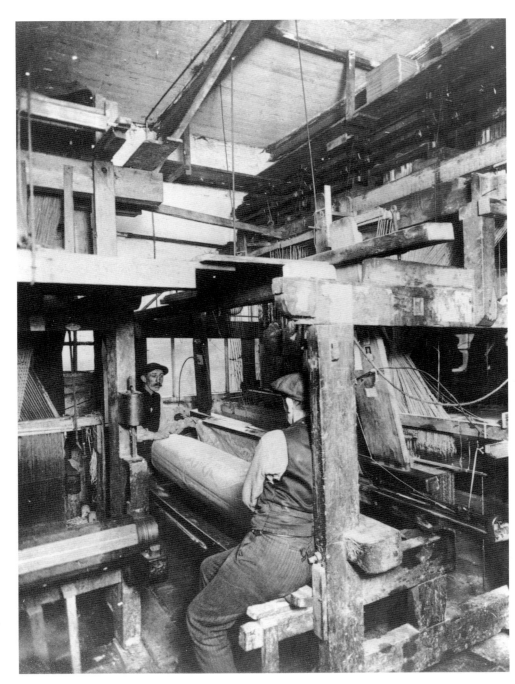

Damask linen being removed
from the cloth beam on a
Coulson tablecloth loom in
1925. The roll of cloth, in a
'brown state', would be sent for
bleaching and beetling before
being cut, hemmed and boxed,
ready for sale. A.R. HOGG, ILC & LM

Redmond Jefferson's noted hardware store in Bow Street, 1926. Included (*left to right*) are: S. Campbell, David McClean, Albert Dillon, Joe Kincaid (Cregan Brothers). Redmond Jefferson continued to trade at this site, in enlarged premises, until the 1980s. Such traditional shops, owned or managed by local families, played an important part in maintaining the town's distinctive identity in an age before the high-street chain store invaded Bow Street. ILC & LM

The Island mill spinning and twisting department. Overlooker Alan McMullan (in the white coat) was, like many others, a life-time employee. He commenced employment in 1900, aged thirteen, and retired in 1952. ILC & LM

Looking down the River Lagan across canal barges moored at the town quay. The Island
Spinning Mill, with its high chimney and four-storey spinning mill, is clearly in view.
Stannus Place, a fine three-storey Georgian terrace built about 1750 (partially hidden behind
the later mill houses), was demolished in the late 1970s. ILC & LM

The dry dock at Quay Street with repair man Danny Kerr on board the lighter *Ruby*. The dock could accommodate at least two vessels and was built by Henry Mulholland, a Lisburn timber merchant, in 1837. It was still in use over a century later and was only filled in when the construction of Queen's Road obliterated Quay Street in 1977. *BELFAST TELEGRAPH*

The motor boat *Nellie of Hilden* passing Barbour's mill on the Lagan navigation in the 1920s.
Traffic on the canal gradually declined during the inter-war years and the waterway was
finally closed in the mid-1950s. ILC & LM

The Belfast Omnibus Company office in Castle Street. In 1927 the BOC absorbed the Classic Bus Company, owned by William Jellie, and the Violet Bus Service, started by James Crothers and Alexander Duggan of Lisburn, and provided a service until its merger into the Northern Ireland Road Transport Board in 1935. Such mergers were a feature of the rapidly expanding bus services of the inter-war years. ILC & LM

Victor Dornan, manager of Lisburn Picture House, which opened in Market Square in 1927, closes up on 6 June 1930. The photograph is a frame from *Lisburn Shopping Week*, a promotional film which was shown in the cinema the following week, along with *Name the Woman*, the silent film advertised. Talkies were first introduced two months later but an accidental fire destroyed this picture house in February 1931. ILC & LM

At work in the Hilden Mill netting sheds in the 1930s. The use of powerloom netting machinery after 1905 allowed Barbour's to expand the production of netting for sea fishing and other purposes. After the Second World War synthetic fibre nets were produced until net-making at Hilden was discontinued about 1960. ILC & LM

The Prince of Wales (later Edward VIII) visited Hilden Mill on 18 November 1932 while on a visit to Northern Ireland to open the new Parliament Buildings at Stormont, and is here seen approaching the decorated entrance of the 'netting department' escorted by John Milne Barbour (*left*) and Malcolm Gordon, his cousin, a director of the Linen Thread Company and manager of Barbour's Hilden and Dunmurry mills. ILC & LM

Opposite: A group of mill girls having fun during the Prince of Wales's visit to Hilden in 1932. Half a century later Mrs Elizabeth Graham (second left) recalled this day as the most memorable of her thirty-eight years working as a reeler in the mill. ILC & LM

Above: Mill Street, Hilden, congested by the workers of William Barbour and Sons (the total workforce was reported at around two thousand employees) who surged around the Prince of Wales's car to see him on his way, 18 November 1932. ILC & LM

In the 1930s the annual Lisburn Chamber of Commerce dinner took place in the Assembly Room. On this occasion in November 1932 the Duke of Abercorn, governor of Northern Ireland, was the principal speaker. At the top table standing (*left to right*) are: H.A. Dornan, G.B. Hanna, James Duff, the Duke of Abercorn, A.K. Harvey, J. Milne Barbour, the Reverend D. Hay and T.J. Russell. The editor of the *Lisburn Standard*, J.F. Burns, is seated directly in front of A.K. Harvey, president of the chamber. ILC & LM (*BELFAST TELEGRAPH*)

The Derry arch in Market Square as the 'Black' procession is halted for a symbolic opening
of the gates by the president of the Lisburn branch of the Apprentice Boys, 26 August 1933.
Thousands of spectators thronged the square to enjoy the parade. ILC & LM

The Horse Fair, Lisburn.

Copyright (25807) Coon, Moira.

The horse fair at Market Place in the 1930s, which drew crowds on fair days to witness the banter and the barter as the horses and ponies were trotted around. Lisburn served as a country market town with separate markets for cattle, poultry, butter, eggs and pork until the middle of the twentieth century. ILC & LM

King George VI and Queen Elizabeth inspect the local members of the British Legion in
Market Square in July 1937, the year of their coronation. The king is accompanied by the
president of the Lisburn legion, Lieutenant Colonel Dr J.G. Johnston MC, and the queen is
escorted by the chairman of Lisburn Urban District Council, J.D. Barbour. ILC & LM

The helmeted firemen of Lisburn Fire Brigade with their new Dennis fire engine purchased by the district council in 1938. The men, and this engine, were involved in major wartime service in the aftermath of the Belfast blitz in 1941. Shortly after, they became a part of the National Fire Service and operated from Abador fire station, a house in Clonevin Park.

McCLEAVE, LHS COLLECTION, ILC & LM

Established in 1910, Duff's was one of several furniture-making factories in the County Down area of Lisburn. From 1942 the company contributed to the war effort by making wings for Short Stirling bombers, while the Hopkins and McCarter factories began making utility furniture to wartime standards in 1944. ILC & LM

121

Above: Magheralave House at the time of its purchase by the War Office in June 1938. Renamed Thiepval Barracks, as a tribute to the Ulster Division's great battle at the Somme, it replaced Victoria Barracks in Belfast as the British army headquarters in Northern Ireland. The house had been built by Thomas Stannus in the last decade of the nineteenth century. *BELFAST TELEGRAPH*

Opposite: Two members of the Royal Welsh Fusiliers walking past the junction of Linenhall Street (*left*) towards Market Square or to the entry to Barnsley's Row on the right. The 4th Battalion was posted to Lisburn on the outbreak of war in 1939 and these soldiers were given temporary billets in the cathedral hall. This area of old housing is associated with Coulson's damask manufactory, the corner of which is just visible on the left, and was demolished in the 1960s to make way for road realignment and the building of a health centre in the 1970s. ILC & LM

1940s

Flax supplies were vital to the war effort and increased production was encouraged by the government. Miss Gardiner, Mrs S. Devlin and Mrs A.F. Main (both née Martin) are shown here demonstrating new flax-pulling machinery at Patrick Gardiner's farm, Ballintine townland, near the Hillsborough Old Road, in August 1940. ILC & LM (*BELFAST TELEGRAPH*)

Children 'do their bit' collecting scrap metal for the war effort at Hillsborough Old Road,
c. 1940. *Left to right*: Bessie Clelland, Jean Clelland, Eddie Lavery (holding the flag), Bobby
Brown, Eadie Clelland, Ethel Semple, Doris Brown and Robert Alexander. ILC & LM
(*BELFAST TELEGRAPH*)

125

The Local Defence Volunteers on parade in Market Square, 1940–1, in black denim uniforms necessitated by the national shortage of khaki. After the fall of France, the LDV, nicknamed the 'look, duck and vanish' brigade, were organised throughout the United Kingdom as a last line of defence. In April 1941 they were issued with army battledress and soon after were renamed the Home Guard. ILC & LM

Women on the home front: members of the Women's Auxiliary Services meeting at Nissen huts in Warren Gardens, 1941. Included are (*left to right*): Miss Scott; Dr May Quinn, MOH; R. Gibson, ARP; a member of the Red Cross; H. Houghton; Mrs Brown, Red Cross; Mrs Deans, WVS; J.D. Barbour, Lisburn Urban District Council; Maureen Crothers, WVS; Mrs Isobel King, WVS; and Mrs G. Gillespie, WVS. ILC & LM (*BELFAST TELEGRAPH*)

Prepared for total war: *above:* Lisburn's Decontamination Squad, a unit of Air Raid Precautions, was trained in basic measures against the effects of gas contamination. They are shown in Wallace Avenue with their squad leader, Fred Kee, second from the right. Shown *opposite* are Lisburn Civil Defence Food Treatment Service out on manoeuvres in light-hearted mood. ILC & LM

Lisburn-born Brigadier Nelson Russell MC, DSO (*right*), commander of the Irish Brigade in North Africa and Italy, in consultation with General (later Field Marshal) Sir Harold Alexander on active service in Tunisia, 1943. Brigadier Russell, who played cricket and hockey for Ireland in the 1920s, was awarded the DSO for his command of the ad hoc Y Division in Tunisia. ILC & LM

Saturday 13 May 1944: the launch of the Salute the Soldier fundraising week of activities in Market Square, presided over by James Duff, chairman of the County Antrim and Lisburn Savings Committees. Lisburn's total of £207,437 raised for the war effort was an impressive achievement. ILC & LM

Field Marshal Sir Bernard Montgomery wearing his famous black beret, addressing soldiers in Thiepval Barracks, 13 September 1945. Monty, who arrived at Long Kesh aerodrome, received a hero's welcome from a large crowd as he drove through the streets of the town on his way to the barracks. He was given the freedom of the city of Belfast the following day. ILC & LM

Lisburn Girls' Training Corps on church parade in Wallace Avenue, *c.* 1946. At the front
(*left to right*) are: Kitty Watson (later Lewis), Nora Allen (later Callaby) and Meta Christie
(later Greer). The corps was inaugurated during the war to give training to girls before entry
into the services. The Princess Royal opened its Lisburn headquarters in the summer of
1945. ILC & LM

Lisburn and District Hospital in the 1940s. This had previously been the Union Workhouse, built in 1845, the last and much-dreaded place of refuge for the poor. The front block was demolished in the 1960s, but its distinctive basalt stone central block remains in use by the Lagan Valley Hospital. ILC & LM

Lisburn-based volunteer firemen of the Southern Fire Authority, with their Dennis light four, in action at a fire on 17 June 1949 that seriously damaged the upper floors of the building in the centre of Market Square. The repaired structure, renamed the Ulster Buildings, survived until its demolition for the new Irish Linen Centre at Lisburn Museum in 1992, coincidentally the same year that the Dennis (sold in 1952) returned to the council's ownership by becoming part of the museum collection. ILC & LM

1950s

Queen Elizabeth II is presented with a bouquet by three-year-old Anne Irwin outside the Assembly Rooms, Market Square, on the occasion of her coronation tour visit with the Duke of Edinburgh, 1 July 1953. The chairman of Lisburn Urban District Council, A.N. Stevenson, is in attendance. LISBURN CAMERA CLUB, ILC & LM

The band of the King's Own Scottish Borderers playing in Market Square on the occasion of
the royal visit, 1 July 1953. LISBURN CAMERA CLUB, ILC & LM

Lisburn railway station staff pose beside the train that was to carry Queen Elizabeth and Prince Philip to Lough Foyle to board the royal yacht, 3 July 1953. ILC & LM

Lisburn actress Mina Dornan, daughter of cinema manager Victor Dornan, was well known for her role as Mrs McCooey in the popular Ulster radio programme *The McCooeys* in the 1950s. She later served the community as the registrar of births, marriages and deaths at the town hall in Castle Street.

BBC NORTHERN IRELAND

The Territorial Army centre in Wallace Avenue, opened by Lady Brookeborough, wife of the prime minister of Northern Ireland, in the presence of Lord Glentoran, colonel of the 6th Battalion, Royal Ulster Rifles, Territorial Army, 23 March 1957.

BELFAST TELEGRAPH

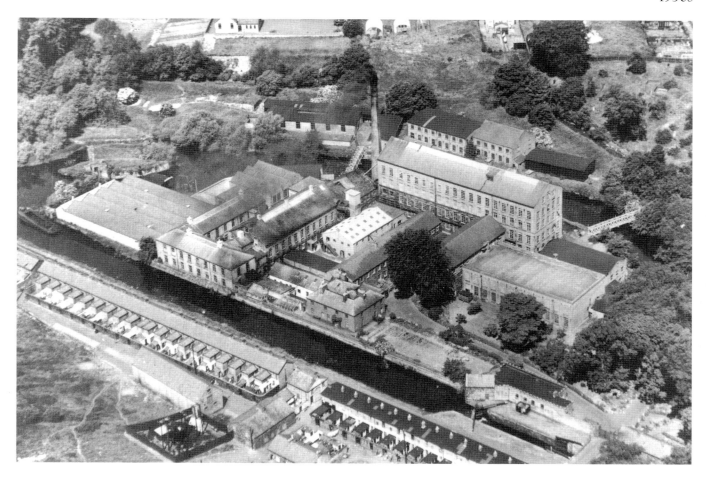

The Island Spinning Mill viewed from the air in the 1950s. The straight waterway was the
Lagan navigation, with its lock gates and mid-eighteenth-century lock-keeper's house
detached from the later mill houses on Canal Street. The site enclosed between the river and
the canal was originally known as Vitriol Island because of the chemical produced there for
bleaching linen. The nineteenth-century four-storey spinning mill and the saw-edged roofed
weaving sheds are clearly visible. The Island Mill, famous for its linen thread, finally ceased
production in 1983. The buildings were demolished in the early 1990s only a short time
before Lisburn Borough Council purchased the site for new civic offices and an arts centre.
The foundation stone of the new building on the renamed Lagan Valley Island, with
restored canal and lock gates, was laid on 12 January 2000 by the mayor, Councillor
Peter O'Hagan. ILC & LM

A view of the RUC station (*left*), the Technical College (Castle House, *centre*), and its annex (*right*), with the war memorial in the foreground as seen from Castle Gardens in the 1950s. This historic area of Lisburn townscape retained the stylish symmetry of its architectural design until the demolition of the Georgian houses on the east side (*right*) of Castle House in the early 1960s for a new hall adjoining the college. GILBERT CAMBLIN

A view of the nineteenth-century black stone houses in Sloan Street as seen through an Orange arch in the 1950s. Most of these houses were demolished or altered beyond recognition in the last quarter of the twentieth century. This photograph was published in Mavis Heaney's *Lisburn Life in the County Down* (1996), a book that highlights the strong community identity of the people who lived and worked in this neighbourhood of Lisburn on the south side of the River Lagan. ILC & LM

1960s

The motorcar, an ever-increasing phenomenon in twentieth-century towns, provided Lisburn with major traffic flow and parking problems until the opening of the M1 motorway in the early 1960s allowed traffic on the east–west and north–south routes to bypass the town centre. This 1960 photograph shows the new one-way system from Bow Street through Market Square. *BELFAST TELEGRAPH*

Lisburn traffic congestion in busy Bow Street, 1960s. *BELFAST TELEGRAPH*

Rebuilt after a fire, the Picture House in Market Square opened in February 1932 with Oscar Hammerstein's *Viennese Nights* and remained a popular place of entertainment until the 1960s. It closed at the end of May 1969, when the final film shown was *The Thomas Crown Affair* starring Steve McQueen and Faye Dunaway. ILC & LM

A train on fire viewed from Harmony Hill in the last days of steam during the 1960s. The Hilden Mill chimney is still pouring out smoke and linen can be seen on the bleach green of the Glenmore Bleach Works. LHS COLLECTION, ILC & LM

The town hall (*right*) and Castle Street (viewed from its front steps) under arctic conditions: the 'big snow' in early 1963 brought terribly difficult conditions. H.A. DUFF, ILC & LM

Lisburn was created a municipal borough in 1964, a historic landmark in the town's history, with the Urban District Council becoming Lisburn Borough Council. The new mayor, Alderman James Howard, in his robes of office and mayoral chain presented by the Linen Thread Company, is seen leaving the cathedral service that celebrated the event on 30 June 1964. He is accompanied by the governor of Northern Ireland, Lord Wakehurst. ILC & LM (*ULSTER STAR*)

The new municipal borough of Lisburn from the air, 1964: 1 gas works; 2 Quay Street and
the town quay; 3 disused dry dock; 4 Assembly Rooms; 5 cathedral; 6 Castle Gardens;
7 Technical College (under development); 8 convent, Castle Street; 9 railway station;
10 courthouse; 11 cycle track in Wallace Park; 12 Friends' School. AEROFILMS

The unveiling of new memorial bronze plaques to the French Huguenot Louis Crommelin (1652-1727) in front of the original Crommelin-De la Cherois headstones in Lisburn cathedral graveyard, 3 August 1964. Included (*left to right*) are: Mrs A.M. Labouchère (née Crommelin), Minister of Finance John Andrews MP, who unveiled the plaques, Sir William Scott, chairman of the Central Council of the Irish Linen Industry, Mrs G.M. Stone (née De la Cherois), Sir Graham Larmor, Frederick Labouchère, and Captain R.M. Crommelin.
R. CLEMENTS LYTTLE, ILC & LM

Parish priest of Lisburn, Canon Thomas McAuley, on the occasion in 1967 of the celebration of the diamond jubilee of his ordination. Born in Glenariff, County Antrim, in 1881, Canon McAuley was then the oldest-serving priest in the diocese of Down and Connor. He was parish priest of Lisburn from 1946 until his death in 1978.

ILC & LM (*ULSTER STAR*)

A view of Bridge Street in the 1960s showing the character of the eighteenth-century houses, many with their original sash windows and nineteenth-century shop fronts. Some of the owners of these businesses continued to live 'over the shop' until the bombing of the town centre during the Troubles led to the final desertion of the upper floors and a consequent decline in the good maintenance of the properties. *BELFAST TELEGRAPH*

The stone backs of the old houses on the south side of Bridge Street as viewed from a new car park created in the mid-1960s after the closure of the gas works. A decade later the provision of an extended car park for the new health centre in Linenhall Street unfortunately led to the demolition of the middle of this intact terrace of three-storey houses and in part ruined a delightful streetscape of great age and character. Tree ring-dating by Queen's University Belfast, of oak structural timbers taken from the demolished 34 Bridge Street, revealed that the houses on this side of the street were built soon after the great fire of Lisburn in 1707. H.A. DUFF, ILC & LM

Samuel Semple (*right*), secretary of the new Lisburn Chamber of Commerce established in 1961, headmaster of Lisnagarvey Boys' Secondary School and a future mayor of the borough (1979–81), photographed in February 1968 discussing a plan for Lisburn's commercial development with Jack Booth, president of the chamber and owner of a decorator's shop in Castle Street. *BELFAST TELEGRAPH*

The Presbyterian Meeting House, or 'First Lisburn' as it became known after the establishment of Railway Street Presbyterian congregation in the mid-nineteenth century, had been entered by an alleyway between houses fronting onto Market Square since the seventeenth century. As this photograph from the mid-1960s shows, the side of the church was only visible from Market Street. H.A. DUFF, ILC & LM

In 1968, at the bicentenary celebrations of the present 'First Lisburn' church buildings and tercentenary of the founding of the congregation, it was decided that 'a visible church would be an advantage in this age of widespread indifference'. As a result, the properties shown in the photograph above were demolished and a new stone frontage, to a design by architect Gordon McKnight, was added. At the dedication of the new extension on 14 June 1970, Dr William Boyd, minister since 1950, was given principal thanks for its inspiration. H.A. DUFF, ILC & LM

The parabolic arches of Lisburn's new swimming pool under construction in 1967. The pool, opened in 1970 by the governor of Northern Ireland, Lord Grey of Naunton, was a fine example of modern architecture, rare in Lisburn. It was demolished in 2000 after the opening of a new pool at the Lagan Valley LeisurePlex. *BELFAST TELEGRAPH*

The front elevation of the new swimming pool as viewed in 1970 from Market Place. *BELFAST TELEGRAPH*

1970-73

Lisnagarvey Hockey Club, under the captainship of David McClements (front centre, holding the flag), at the opening ceremony of the European Club Championships in the Olympic Stadium, Rome, Easter 1971. In the 1970-1 season 'Garvey' won the Irish Senior Cup, the Kirk Cup and became British club champions, a title they retained the following year. SERGIO FERRI, ROME, ILC & LM

The mayor, Hugh G. Bass, observes James Callaghan, Labour shadow home secretary and future prime minister, signing the visitors' book in the town hall, 26 March 1971. Callaghan congratulated the town on its fine appearance, low rate of unemployment and history of peace. *ULSTER STAR*

Mayoress Joan Bass presents a shield to boys of St Aloysius Primary School (Ballinderry Road), winners of a five-a-side soccer competition in Festival Fair, an event organised by Lisburn Chamber of Commerce in 1971. 'St Ally's', as it was known to the children, replaced the long-established Lisburn Boys' School at Chapel Hill in 1968, and with new facilities set an enviable record of sporting achievement. A principal of both schools, Brendan Fitzpatrick, had served as treasurer of the Lisburn Schools' Football League from 1936 to 1970, an important organisation which had ensured that schoolchildren from different traditions met on the playing field. His successor as principal, Peter O'Hagan, a teacher at Lisburn Boys' since 1952, later served the league as honorary secretary. GEORGE BAXTER, ILC & LM

Devastation in Bow Street after a terrorist car bomb explosion, 14 March 1972. The frequency of such attacks in the 1970s caused the *Ulster Star* to describe the street with the front page headline – 'Bomb Alley'. *BELFAST TELEGRAPH*

Mayor Hugh G. Bass was awarded the freedom of the borough at a ceremony held in the Assembly Rooms on 26 September 1973. He is seen showing the scroll that confirmed his rights as an honorary burgess to (*left to right*): Aldermen J.D. Black and J. Dickey, Councillor David Shanks and Aldermen Samuel Higgins and James Howard. This was the last major civic event in the life of the first Lisburn Borough Council, which ceased to function on 1 October 1973. *ULSTER STAR*

Select Bibliography

Bannister, R.C., and R.V. Hamilton, *Sport in Lisburn, Past and Present*, Belfast, 1910

Barton, Brian, *Northern Ireland in the Second World War*, Belfast, 1995

Bass, H.G., *Boyd's of Castle Buildings, Lisburn: A Short History of an Old Family Firm*, Lisburn, 1977

Bassett, G.H., *The Book of Antrim: A Manual and Directory*, Dublin, 1888; reprinted as *County Antrim 100 Years Ago*, Belfast, 1988

Bayly, Henry, *A Topographical and Historical Account of Lisburn . . .*, Belfast, 1834

Blair, May, *Once Upon the Lagan: The Story of the Lagan Canal*, Belfast, 1981

Brett, C.E.B., and Lady Dunleath, *List of Historic Buildings . . . in the Borough of Lisburn*, Belfast, 1969

Camblin, Gilbert, *The Town in Ulster*, Belfast, 1951

Carmody, W.P., *Lisburn Cathedral and its Past Rectors*, Belfast, 1926

Collins, Brenda, *Flax to Fabric*, Lisburn, 1994

Craig, W.I., *Presbyterianism in Lisburn from the Seventeenth Century*, Belfast, 1960

Crawford, W.H., 'Lisburn at the coming of the Huguenots' and 'The Huguenots and the linen industry' in W.A. Maguire (ed.), *The Huguenots and Ulster 1685–1985*, Lisburn, 1985

Day, Angélique, and Patrick McWilliams (eds), *Ordnance Survey Memoirs of Ireland*, vol. 8, *Parishes of County Antrim II 1832–8*, Belfast, 1991

Doherty, Richard, *Irish Generals in the British Army in the Second World War*, Belfast, 1993

Green, E.R.R., *The Lagan Valley 1800–1850: A Local History of the Industrial Revolution*, London, 1949

    'The cotton hand-loom weavers in north-east Ireland' in *Ulster Journal of Archaeology*, 1944

    'Thomas Barbour and the American linen-thread industry' in J.M. Goldstrom and L.A. Clarkson (eds), *Irish Population, Economy and Society*, Oxford, 1981

[Greene, W.J.], *A Concise History of Lisburn and Neighbourhood*, Belfast, 1906

Hamilton, R.W., *A Short Family and Personal History*, with notes by J.V. Hamilton, n.p., n.d.

Hickey, Kieran, *The Light of Other Days: Irish Life at the Turn of the Century in the Photographs of Robert French*, London, 1973

Hughes, Peter, *The Founders of the Wallace Collection*, London, 1981

Kee, Fred, *Lisburn Miscellany*, Lisburn, 1976

Lisburn Herald, 1891–1969

Lisburn Historical Society Journal, I (1979) – IX (1995), particularly the articles in the following volumes:

    III, Burns, J.F., 'The life and work of Sir Richard Wallace Bart. MP';

    IV, Dixon, Hugh, 'Aspects of the legacy of Sir Richard Wallace in the fabric of Lisburn';

    V, Burns, J.F., 'Jigging to the fiddle at Hilden – an infamous Lisburn by-election recalled;

    VI, Mackey, Brian, 'The market house and Assembly Rooms, Lisburn';

    VII, Gillespie, Raymond, 'George Rawdon's Lisburn';

    VIII, McReynolds, Alister, 'The establishment of technical education in Lisburn'; and McNeill, D.B., 'Lisburn bus services in the 1920s and '30s'

Lisburn Standard, 1876–1959

Macaulay, Ambrose, *Convent of the Sacred Heart of Mary, Lisburn, 1870–1970*, n.p., n.d.

McCarrison, J.H.F., *Lisburn Golf Club 1905–1980*, Lisburn, 1980

Mackey, Brian, 'Centres of drawloom damask linen weaving in Ireland in the 18th and 19th centuries' in *Riggisberger Berichte* 7, Riggisberg, 1999

Newhouse, N.H., *A History of Friends' School, Lisburn*, n.p., 1974

O'Laverty, James, *An Historical Account of the Diocese of Down and Connor*, Dublin, 1880; reissued, Spa, 1981

Orr, G.E., *Lisburn Methodism*, Lisburn, 1975

[Samuels, A.P.I. and D.G.S.], *With the Ulster Division in France: A Story of the 11th Battalion Royal Irish Rifles (South Antrim Volunteers)*, Belfast, n.p., n.d.

Ulster Star, 1957–

Urquhart, Diane, *Women in Ulster Politics 1890–1940*, Dublin, 2000

Walker, B.M., *Ulster Politics: The Formative Years, 1868–1886*, Belfast, 1989